Chicago Deal Flow

Financing Your Real Estate Investment

Michael Linton

Chicago Deal Flow: Financing Your Real Estate Investment

ISBN: 9798871551301

Published by Michael Linton

Imprint: Independently published

Cover design by Michael Linton

Interior layout and design by Michael Linton

Printed in the USA

First Edition: November 2023

Michael Linton, NCREA, CREIPS
ChicagoDealFlow.com

For permission requests, write to the publisher at
michael@lintonglobal.com

This book is a work of nonfiction. Names, characters, places, and incidents are the product of the author's actual experience. Any resemblance to actual events, locales, or persons, living or dead, is entirely coincidental.

Visit our website at ChicagoDealFlow.com

Manufactured in the USA

Printed on acid-free paper

Dedication

To my Savior, Jesus Christ:

With humble gratitude, I offer you this work, a testament to your unwavering guidance and infinite grace. Your light has illuminated my path, leading me through every challenge and blessing. For your constant presence, I am eternally grateful.

To my beloved wife and partner, Peggy Linton:

Your unwavering support and insightful wisdom are the bedrock upon which I stand. This book is a tribute to the incredible partnership we share, forever intertwined in love and collaboration.

Table of Contents

Legal Disclaimer

As a seasoned commercial broker and real estate investor with 37 years in the industry, I've garnered invaluable insights and experiences that I'm eager to share with you in this book. However, it's vitally important that I commence with a legal disclaimer. While the knowledge and strategies I present are drawn from my long-standing experience, the following pages should not be construed as providing legal, financial, or professional advice.

The realm of real estate investing is intricate and multifaceted. Each property, deal, and situation comes with its unique circumstances. While I've endeavored to deliver precise and up-to-date information, it should be seen as a general guideline or a foundation upon which to build, not as an exhaustive or personalized plan.

Even though I've done my utmost to ensure the information's accuracy at the time of writing, keep in mind that real estate markets are dynamic. Economic conditions, market trends, zoning laws, tax implications, and many other factors influencing a real estate investment can change. Given this fluidity, some details and advice might become less relevant or outdated over time.

Moreover, Chicago, like all cities, has its unique regulations and market specifics. Although many of the principles and strategies I share may have broader applicability, some might be particularly relevant to the Chicagoland market and less so to other locales.

The successes I've enjoyed, which I will share with you, stem from meticulous planning, rigorous research, risk mitigation, and, at times, a little serendipity. Real estate investment involves substantial financial risk, and it is possible to lose part or all of your investment. Therefore, I implore you to seek advice from a certified professional - a lawyer, financial advisor, or real estate professional - before making significant investment decisions.

While this book discusses various investment strategies, their inclusion should not be seen as an endorsement. Each investor must assess their financial situation, risk tolerance, and investment objectives before choosing their course.

Finally, remember that real estate investing, like all worthwhile endeavors, demands dedication, patience, and continuous learning. Success rarely happens overnight; often, it's the product of consistency and resilience amid setbacks.

By proceeding with this book, you acknowledge that I - the author, broker, and investor - cannot be held liable for any

decisions you make based on the information provided. You agree to accept all risks linked to real estate investments and understand it is your responsibility to conduct thorough due diligence and consult with professionals as necessary.

With that necessary preamble, I am thrilled to start this journey with you, sharing the strategies, insights, and experiences that have steered my fulfilling career in the vibrant, challenging, yet ultimately rewarding world of real estate investing in Chicago.

Welcome to ChicagoDealFlow.com:

Your Gateway to Real Estate Prosperity

Greetings, fellow investors, and welcome to ChicagoDealFlow.com, your premier resource for unlocking the boundless potential of real estate investment in Chicago and its vibrant suburbs.

I'm Michael Linton, and I'm honored to be your guide on this exciting journey through the ever-evolving world of real estate investment. With nearly four decades of experience in the industry, I've made it my mission to share the insights, strategies, and wisdom I've gathered along the way to help you prosper in Chicago's dynamic real estate market.

A Wealth of Investment Opportunities

Chicago, often dubbed the "City of Big Shoulders," offers a landscape ripe with investment prospects. From the heart of downtown to the tranquil suburbs, this city has something for every investor. Whether you're eyeing residential properties, commercial spaces, or vacant land, you'll find an array of opportunities to explore and leverage for your financial growth.

Comprehensive Investment Insights

At ChicagoDealFlow.com, we go beyond the basics. We delve deep into the intricate art of real estate investment. Our blog is your treasure trove of knowledge, filled with expert advice, market trends, and insider tips that can make all the difference in your investment journey. Whether you're a seasoned pro or just starting, our articles are crafted to empower you with the latest insights and strategies.

Real Estate Listings at Your Fingertips

As an investor, access to accurate and up-to-date listings is invaluable. That's why we provide IDX listings that cover residential, commercial, and vacant land properties throughout the Chicago area. You can explore these listings at your leisure, filtering them to match your investment goals, and discover the gems that align with your vision.

Exclusive Private Listings

In addition to IDX listings, we offer a selection of private listings that aren't available on public platforms. These off-market opportunities can be the key to securing prime properties before they hit the mainstream market. It's just one more way we help you stay ahead of the competition.

Chicago Deal Flow: Financing Your Real Estate Investment

Educational Investment Videos

Knowledge is power, and we believe in empowering our community of investors. That's why we feature a library of investment videos covering a wide range of topics. Whether you're interested in market analysis, investment strategies, or property management insights, our videos are designed to enrich your understanding and boost your confidence in the world of real estate.

Promoting the Chicago Deal Flow Book Series

We're proud to present the Chicago Deal Flow Book Series, a collection of in-depth guides that delve into the nuances of real estate investment in Chicago and its suburbs. These books are your companions on this journey, offering comprehensive insights, practical advice, and expert perspectives. Whether you're new to the game or a seasoned investor, our book series has something to offer.

(continued next page)

Join the Chicago Deal Flow Community

Investing in real estate is not just a transaction; it's a journey, a journey that we embark on together. ChicagoDealFlow.com is not just a website; it's a community of like-minded individuals, all striving for financial success through real estate investment. We invite you to be a part of this community, to explore, learn, and grow with us.

Thank you for choosing ChicagoDealFlow.com as your trusted resource. We're here to support you in every step of your real estate investment endeavors. As you navigate this site, remember that your success is our success, and we're committed to helping you achieve your investment goals.

Here's to your prosperous future in Chicago's real estate market.

Sincerely,

Michael Linton

Preface

Welcome, fellow investor. Whether you're a seasoned veteran or just dipping your toes into the exciting world of real estate, I'm thrilled to have you here. This book is your guide to navigating the intricate landscape of Chicago's real estate financing, regardless of your investment goals.

At its core, this book stems from a fundamental belief: all real estate is an investment. From the cozy single-family home to the towering commercial complex, each property holds the potential to generate value and cultivate prosperity. Whether it's the roof over your head or the foundation for your business, understanding real estate financing empowers you to build a stronger, more secure future.

Within these pages, you'll find a comprehensive roadmap to unlock the secrets of Chicago's investment landscape. We'll delve into the nuances of financing diverse property types, exploring traditional and alternative solutions that cater to your specific needs. We'll unveil the intricacies of loan programs, decode complex concepts like buydowns and mortgage insurance, and equip you with the tools to

negotiate favorable terms and secure the financing that fuels your ambitions.

This journey is not merely about bricks and mortar; it's about unlocking the potential that lies within each property. It's about building a legacy, brick by brick, and forging a path towards financial security and stability. So, whether you seek to create a comfortable haven for your family or build a thriving investment portfolio, this book is your compass, guiding you through the exciting world of Chicago real estate financing.

Let the adventure begin!

What is Chicago Deal Flow?

In the bustling real estate market of Chicago and its suburbs, the term "Chicago Deal Flow" has become synonymous with strategic and informed investment opportunities. But what exactly does it mean?

At its core, Chicago Deal Flow represents a comprehensive approach to real estate investing in the city. It encompasses identifying profitable opportunities, navigating complex market dynamics, and utilizing effective strategies to maximize returns.

This involves:

Access to exclusive listings and off-market deals: Chicago Deal Flow provides investors with insider access to properties that aren't readily available on the public market, offering the chance to acquire valuable assets before they hit mainstream attention.

Expert market analysis and insights: Navigating the Chicago real estate landscape requires a deep understanding of local trends, neighborhood nuances,

and regulatory requirements. Chicago Deal Flow equips investors with this crucial knowledge, allowing them to make informed decisions based on accurate data and expert analysis.

Building strategic partnerships: Success in the Chicago market often hinges on collaborating with experienced professionals. Chicago Deal Flow facilitates connections with reliable brokers, lenders, and other key stakeholders, providing investors with the support network they need to thrive.

Utilizing proven investment strategies: Chicago Deal Flow delves into various investment strategies tailored to the Chicago market, including fix-and-flip, rental income generation, and long-term value appreciation. Investors gain valuable insights into these strategies, enabling them to choose the approach that best aligns with their goals.

Whether you're a seasoned investor or a newcomer to the Chicago market, understanding and leveraging Chicago Deal Flow can be the key to unlocking your real estate investment potential. It empowers you to navigate the complexities of the market, identify lucrative opportunities, and make informed decisions that lead to success.

Chapter 1: The Chicago Real Estate Landscape: A Tapestry of Opportunity

Imagine yourself soaring above the iconic Chicago skyline, the wind whipping through your hair as you take in the breathtaking panorama below. Towering skyscrapers pierce the clouds, while charming neighborhoods unfold like vibrant mosaics, each with its own unique personality and charm. This is Chicago, a city where history and innovation collide, tradition and progress coexist, and opportunity whispers its secrets on the wind.

For the astute investor, Chicago's real estate landscape is a canvas teeming with possibilities, waiting to be painted with the vibrant colors of success. Whether you seek the warmth and stability of a single-family home nestled within a historic neighborhood like Lincoln Park, or the breathtaking views and cosmopolitan lifestyle offered by a sleek high-rise in the heart of the Loop, Chicago has something for every taste and ambition.

But Chicago's appeal goes beyond mere aesthetics. It's a city that pulsates with the energy of commerce, where bustling retail districts like Magnificent Mile and

vibrant business hubs like Fulton Market drive the engine of the city's economy. For those with an eye for the future, the development scene offers a tantalizing glimpse into the city's ever-evolving landscape, with innovative projects like Lincoln Yards and The 78 reshaping the skyline and presenting exciting opportunities for capitalizing on the city's growth.

Yet, beneath the surface of this dynamic metropolis lies a complex network of regulations and economic forces that shape the market. Understanding this intricate interplay is crucial for navigating the sometimes-challenging waters of real estate financing. Zoning regulations, like those governing the historic districts of Wicker Park or Hyde Park, ensure harmonious development while preserving the character of each neighborhood. Building codes, meticulously crafted to guarantee the safety and integrity of structures, become the guardians of your investment's longevity. And taxation, an inevitable factor in any investment landscape, requires careful consideration to optimize your financial strategy.

However, the future of Chicago's real estate market shines bright. A robust economy, fueled by job creation and a thriving business climate, continues to drive demand for both residential and commercial

properties. Technology, the ever-present force of change, is transforming the industry, with innovative platforms like ChicagoDealFlow.com and Zillow streamlining the search for investment opportunities and facilitating seamless communication between buyers and sellers. And as sustainability becomes increasingly ingrained in our collective consciousness, the demand for energy-efficient buildings like those in The Green Exchange and LEED-certified structures presents exciting possibilities for eco-conscious investors.

Whether you're a seasoned veteran or a budding entrepreneur, Chicago's real estate landscape beckons you with its rich tapestry of opportunities. With its diverse offerings, vibrant economy, and ever-evolving future, this city offers a unique platform for building your legacy, brick by brick, one investment at a time. So, take a deep breath, embrace the wind of change, and embark on your own Chicago real estate adventure. The Windy City awaits, ready to reward your vision and audacity.

Chapter 2: Understanding Real Estate Financing Basics

In the realm of real estate investment, understanding the fundamentals of financing is akin to laying a strong foundation for a building. Without a solid grasp of financing, any real estate investment strategy is at risk of crumbling under the weight of unforeseen challenges and market dynamics. This chapter aims to provide an insightful and informative overview of real estate financing, particularly within the context of the vibrant Chicago market.

The Essence of Real Estate Financing

Real estate financing involves securing funds to purchase or develop property. It's a critical tool for investors, enabling them to leverage their capital to acquire assets that might otherwise be beyond their immediate financial reach. The key to successful real estate financing lies in selecting the right financing method that aligns with your investment goals and risk tolerance.

Types of Real Estate Financing

Several financing options are available to real estate investors, each with its unique characteristics and requirements:

Conventional Mortgages: Standard loans provided by banks and other financial institutions, often requiring a down payment of around 20% of the property's purchase price. They offer relatively lower interest rates compared to other options. Some conventional loans will let you have a down payment as little as 5%. Always talk to a loan officer for details.

Government-Insured Loans: Loans like those insured by the Federal Housing Administration (FHA) or the Veterans Administration (VA), often requiring lower down payments and having less stringent credit requirements. Useful for first-time homebuyers or those who might not qualify for conventional mortgages.

Hard Money Loans: Short-term loans with higher interest rates, often used by investors looking to renovate and flip properties quickly. Secured by the

property itself and typically funded by private investors or companies.

Private Money Loans: Similar to hard money loans but involve borrowing from individual investors or groups. The terms are often negotiable, and the loan is secured by the real estate asset.

Commercial Loans: Tailored to meet the unique needs of commercial real estate investments. They often have different terms and requirements compared to residential loans.

Assessing Your Financing Options

When choosing a financing option, consider factors like:

> Interest rate: The cost of borrowing the money.
> Term: The length of the loan.
> Amortization period: The timeframe for paying off the loan.
> Fees and penalties: Additional costs associated with the loan.

It's crucial to match the loan type to your investment strategy. For example, a short-term hard money loan might be appropriate for a flip, while a long-term conventional mortgage might be better suited for a rental property.

Navigating the Chicago Financing Landscape: Insights for Real Estate Investors

Financing real estate investments in Chicago has its unique nuances. The city's diverse neighborhoods, varying property values, and economic dynamics play a significant role in determining the most suitable financing option.

Market Trends and Impacts:

Chicago's real estate market is influenced by economic trends, population shifts, and urban development policies. Staying informed about these trends can help investors make more informed financing decisions.

Areas undergoing revitalization may offer attractive investment opportunities but may also come with higher risks.

Local Lending Landscape:

Understanding the local lending landscape is crucial. Chicago boasts a mix of national banks, regional banks,and local credit unions, each offering different loan products.

Building relationships with local lenders can be beneficial, as they often have a better understanding of the local market.

Navigating Legal and Regulatory Requirements:

Real estate financing in Chicago is subject to federal, state, and local regulations. Familiarity with these regulations is essential to ensure compliance and avoid legal pitfalls.

This includes understanding zoning laws, property taxes, and compliance with fair housing laws.

The Importance of Professional Guidance:

Consulting with real estate attorneys, mortgage brokers, and financial advisors can provide valuable insights and help navigate the complexities of real estate financing.

These professionals can assist in evaluating loan options, negotiating terms, and ensuring legal compliance.

Conclusion:

Mastering the fundamentals of real estate financing is a crucial step for any investor, especially in a dynamic market like Chicago. By understanding the different types of financing available, assessing your options carefully, and staying informed about market and regulatory conditions, you can make well-informed decisions that align with your investment goals.

As you progress in your real estate investment journey, remember that financing is not just about acquiring funds; it's about strategically leveraging those funds to maximize your investment potential

while managing risks effectively. With the right approach, real estate financing can be a powerful tool in building a successful investment portfolio.

Chapter 3: Navigating the Chicago Real Estate Financing Landscape: Tailoring Strategies by Property Type

In the dynamic Chicago real estate market, navigating the complexities of financing various property types is crucial for investors to maximize their success. This chapter delves into the distinct financing options and considerations for single-family homes, multi-unit buildings, commercial properties, and new construction projects. Each property type presents unique challenges and opportunities, demanding tailored financing strategies to achieve optimal results.

Single-Family Homes:

> Mortgage Options: Conventional loans, readily available through banks and other lenders, are the most common choice. These loans offer fixed or adjustable rates over 15-30 years. FHA loans with lower down payments can be attractive for investor-occupants.

Investment Considerations: Higher down payments (20-25%) are typically required for investment properties.Investors need to assess the property's potential rental income to ensure it covers mortgage payments and operating expenses.

Multi-Unit Buildings:

Loan Types: For buildings with up to four units, residential mortgages (conventional, FHA, VA) are available.Commercial loans are required for larger properties.

Analyzing Cash Flow: Lenders meticulously assess a building's income potential, considering occupancy rates,rental income, and operating expenses. Loan terms are heavily influenced by the projected cash flow.

Unique Challenges: Managing multiple tenants and ensuring consistent rental income can be complex for investors.

Commercial Properties:

Commercial Mortgages: Short-term loans with higher interest rates and balloon payments are common. Loan approval depends on the property's income potential, location, condition, and the borrower's creditworthiness.

Tenant Considerations: The creditworthiness of tenants and lease terms significantly impact the property's financial stability and loan terms.

Specialization: Deep market knowledge and a skilled team are crucial for success in the complex commercial real estate financing landscape.

New Construction:

Construction Loans: These short-term, high-interest loans finance the building phase and convert into traditional mortgages upon completion.

Project Feasibility: Lenders evaluate the developer's experience, project plan, budget, and timeline. Detailed plans and financial projections are critical for securing funding.

Risk Management: Careful planning, experienced partners, and contingency plans are essential to mitigate the inherent risks associated with new construction projects.

Chicago Market Nuances:

Local Lending Landscape: Understanding local banks and credit unions with expertise in specific property types or areas can lead to more favorable loan terms.

Regulatory Environment: Zoning laws, property taxes, and development incentives can impact investment viability and profitability. Staying informed about these regulations is crucial.

Building Relationships: Cultivating relationships with local lenders, brokers, and real estate professionals can provide invaluable insights and support.

Successfully navigating the Chicago real estate financing landscape requires a comprehensive understanding of various property types and their unique financing requirements. Investors must tailor

their strategies to each scenario, considering market conditions, property potential, and available loan options. By mastering these nuances and leveraging local expertise, investors can make informed decisions that drive their portfolio's success in the dynamic Chicago market.

Chapter 4: Unlocking the Vault: Exploring Diverse Loan Options for Real Estate Investment

The world of real estate investment thrives on the ability to unlock its vast financial potential. This chapter serves as your key to the vault, revealing the diverse loan options available to investors, encompassing both established favorites and hidden gems. From the readily accessible FHA loans to the niche portfolio options and alternative financing routes, we'll embark on a comprehensive exploration, equipping you with the knowledge to make informed choices and navigate the complex financial landscape with confidence.

FHA Loans: Demystifying the Benefits, Drawbacks, and Eligibility

The Federal Housing Administration (FHA) loan program has been a cornerstone of American homeownership for over 80 years, helping millions of first-time homebuyers and borrowers with lower credit

scores achieve their dream of owning a home. By offering flexible eligibility requirements, lower down payments, and competitive interest rates, FHA loans have democratized access to homeownership for many Americans. However, like any loan program, FHA loans come with their own set of benefits and drawbacks that potential borrowers should carefully consider before taking the leap.

Benefits of FHA Loans:

Lower Down Payment: Compared to conventional loans, which typically require a 20% down payment, FHA loans require a down payment as low as 3.5% of the purchase price. This significantly reduces the upfront financial burden for borrowers, making homeownership more attainable.

Flexible Credit Requirements: FHA loans are more forgiving of credit blemishes than conventional loans.Borrowers with credit scores as low as 580 may qualify for an FHA loan, opening doors to homeownership for individuals who might otherwise be excluded.

Competitive Interest Rates: While conventional loan rates may offer slightly lower rates, FHA loan rates remain competitive and can be a good option for borrowers who do not have perfect credit.

Streamlined Approval Process: The FHA loan approval process is generally faster and less stringent compared to conventional loans, offering a quicker path to homeownership.

More Flexible Debt-to-Income Ratio: FHA loans allow for a higher debt-to-income (DTI) ratio than conventional loans, making them more accessible to borrowers with other financial obligations.

Drawbacks of FHA Loans:

Mortgage Insurance: FHA loans require borrowers to pay mortgage insurance premiums (MIP) both upfront and monthly. This additional cost can add to the overall loan amount and monthly payments.

Loan Limits: FHA loans have lower loan limits than conventional loans, which can restrict purchase options in high-cost areas.

Higher Interest Rates: While competitive, FHA loan rates can be slightly higher than conventional loan rates for borrowers with good credit scores.

Appraisal Requirements: FHA loans have stricter appraisal requirements, which can sometimes delay the loan process or lead to purchase offers being rejected.

Eligibility Requirements:

To qualify for an FHA loan, borrowers must meet certain minimum requirements:

Credit Score: Minimum credit score of 580, although higher scores may be required for lower down payments.

Debt-to-Income Ratio: DTI ratio should not exceed 43%, although some lenders may consider higher ratios in certain cases.

Employment History: Stable employment history with sufficient income to support the mortgage payments.

Down Payment: Minimum down payment of 3.5% of the purchase price.

Property Requirements: The property must meet FHA appraisal standards and be located in an eligible area.

Loan Limits:

FHA loan limits vary by county and are subject to change annually. In 2023, the maximum loan limit for a single-family home in most areas is $472,030. However, this limit can be higher in certain high-cost areas.

FHA loans offer a valuable pathway to homeownership for many individuals and families. By understanding the benefits and drawbacks, eligibility requirements, and loan limits, borrowers can make an informed decision about whether an FHA loan is the right choice for them. It's crucial to consult with a qualified mortgage professional to assess individual circumstances and explore all available options before embarking on the homeownership journey.

References:

Federal Housing Administration.
https://www.hud.gov/buying/loans. Accessed October 26,
2023.

U.S. Department of Housing and Urban
Development.https://www.hud.gov/program_offices/housing/s
fh/lender/origination/mortgage_limits. Accessed October
26,2023.

The Mortgage Reports.
https://www.hud.gov/program_offices/housing/hsgrroom/fhap
rodrpt. Accessed October 26, 2023.

Chapter 5: Transforming Fixer-Uppers into Dream Homes: The Power of FHA 203(k) Loans

For many aspiring homeowners, the dream of owning a property can be stalled by outdated features or structural issues.Fortunately, the FHA 203(k) loan program offers a powerful solution, merging both home purchase and renovation financing into one streamlined process. This innovative program empowers individuals to acquire a fixer-upper, unlock its hidden potential, and transform it into their ideal home, all while benefiting from the FHA's flexible eligibility requirements and competitive interest rates.

Renovating with Ease:

The FHA 203(k) program encompasses a wide range of renovations, covering both cosmetic upgrades and essential structural repairs. Breathe new life into your property with updates like foundation work, roof replacement, plumbing and electrical upgrades, bathroom additions, kitchen renovations, accessibility features, energy-efficient improvements,and even

non-essential enhancements like swimming pools, landscaping, and patios.

Choosing the Right Fit:

Tailor the program to your specific needs by selecting the loan option that best suits your renovation plans. The Limited 203(k) program covers improvements up to $35,000, ideal for smaller projects. For more extensive renovations, the Standard 203(k) offers flexibility with no upper limit.

Accessibility and Affordability:

Similar to standard FHA loans, the 203(k) program boasts loan limits adjusted annually, typically exceeding those of conventional loans. This translates to greater accessibility and affordability, making your dream home more attainable.In 2023, for instance, the loan limit for a single-family home in most areas sits at $472,030 for both the Standard and Limited 203(k) options.

Unlocking Your Eligibility:

Qualifying for an FHA 203(k) loan is straightforward. Meet the standard FHA requirements, including a minimum credit score of 580 (higher scores may be

required for lower down payments), a debt-to-income ratio not exceeding 43%, sufficient income to support mortgage payments, a down payment of at least 3.5% of the purchase price plus renovation costs, and a property meeting FHA appraisal standards located in an eligible area.

Transforming Your Vision into Reality:

The FHA 203(k) program simplifies your renovation journey by eliminating the need for separate financing for each stage. This streamlined approach makes it an ideal option for first-time homebuyers and anyone seeking to unlock the hidden potential of a fixer-upper.

Expert Guidance for a Smooth Journey:

To ensure a smooth and successful renovation process, partnering with qualified professionals is crucial. Consult with a mortgage expert to navigate the loan application process and a licensed contractor to ensure your chosen improvements are FHA-compliant. Together, they'll help you develop a realistic budget and timeline for your project, turning your renovation dreams into a seamless and rewarding experience.

Beyond Brick and Mortar:

Investing in an FHA 203(k) loan isn't just about renovating a property; it's about transforming your entire lifestyle.Embrace this powerful tool to unlock the door to your dream home, a space tailored to your unique needs and aspirations. Let the FHA 203(k) program be your key to unlocking a world of possibilities and realizing your homeownership dreams.

Chapter 6: Navigating the Financial Landscape: VA Loans for Your Chicago Real Estate Investment

For veterans, service members, and their families, the dream of owning a piece of the vibrant Chicago real estate market becomes a tangible reality with the invaluable support of VA Loans. These government-backed mortgages,guaranteed by the Department of Veterans Affairs, offer a unique blend of benefits, flexible terms, and competitive rates, making them a compelling choice for veterans embarking on their investment journey.

Unlocking the Advantages:

One of the most significant advantages of VA loans is the lower down payment requirement. Unlike conventional loans,which typically require a 20% down payment, VA loans allow qualified veterans to purchase a home with a significantly lower down payment, ranging from 0% to 3.6%. This drastically reduces the upfront financial burden, making homeownership more accessible and attainable for veterans with limited savings.

Furthermore, VA loans boast consistently lower interest rates compared to their conventional counterparts. This

translates to substantial savings over the life of the loan, resulting in lower monthly mortgage payments. This financial advantage allows veterans to invest in a wider range of properties or allocate resources towards other investment goals,further expanding their financial possibilities.

VA loans also stand out for their flexible eligibility requirements. Compared to other loan programs, they offer a broader reach, extending eligibility beyond active-duty service members to veterans who have served honorably in the past, reservists, and National Guard members. This inclusivity opens doors for a wider range of veterans to participate in the Chicago real estate market.

Another key benefit of VA loans is the elimination of private mortgage insurance (PMI). Unlike conventional loans where PMI is mandatory for down payments below 20%, VA loans completely remove this additional monthly expense.This significantly reduces the overall financial burden for veterans, making their loan even more affordable and attractive.

Finally, VA loans are known for their streamlined and efficient application process. Compared to traditional loan options, veterans can expect a faster and less stringent approval process, allowing them to secure their desired

property and begin their investment journey sooner rather than later. This streamlined approach removes unnecessary delays and helps veterans capitalize on valuable opportunities in the dynamic Chicago market.

Recognizing the Considerations:

While VA loans offer a plethora of advantages, it's important to acknowledge some potential drawbacks. One key consideration is the loan limit. These government-backed mortgages are subject to limits set by the Department of Veterans Affairs, which can vary depending on the county and property type. In certain high-cost areas like Chicago,these limits may be lower compared to conforming loan limits for conventional mortgages. This can potentially restrict the purchasing power of veterans in these markets.

Additionally, VA loans require borrowers to pay a funding fee. This fee helps sustain the program and offset the government's risk. While the fee can be financed into the loan, it adds to the overall cost of borrowing and should be factored into the financial equation.

Another consideration involves the stricter property appraisal requirements associated with VA loans. Compared to conventional loans, stricter standards apply

for properties to qualify for VA financing. This may lead to potential delays in the approval process if the property does not meet the VA's standards. Additionally, certain property types, such as manufactured homes, may not be eligible for VA financing.

Charting Your Course:

To qualify for a VA loan, veterans must meet specific eligibility requirements outlined by the Department of Veterans Affairs. These include:

Military Service: Veterans must have served a minimum period of active duty service, adhering to specific requirements based on their branch of service and discharge status.

Character of Service: Veterans must have been discharged under honorable conditions.

Creditworthiness: While offering more flexibility than conventional loans, VA loans still require a responsible credit history. Typically, a minimum credit score ranging from 580 to 620 is expected.

Debt-to-Income Ratio: To ensure they can comfortably manage mortgage payments alongside

other financial obligations, veterans must maintain a healthy debt-to-income ratio, usually not exceeding 43%.

Certificate of Eligibility (COE): Obtaining a Certificate of Eligibility from the Department of Veterans Affairs is crucial for veterans to verify their eligibility for the VA loan program.

Loan Limits: VA loans are subject to limits set by the Department of Veterans Affairs, which can vary depending on the county and property type. While this limit may be sufficient for most areas within Chicago city limits, it's crucial to note that it can be higher for certain high-cost counties within the greater metropolitan area. To determine the specific loan limit applicable to your desired property, it's recommended to consult with a qualified lending institution.

Making Informed Decisions:

VA loans offer a powerful and accessible financial tool for veterans aiming to invest in their future through Chicago's dynamic real estate market. By understanding the benefits, drawbacks, and eligibility requirements, veterans can make informed decisions

about whether this option aligns with their specific investment goals. With their competitive rates, minimal down payment requirements, and streamlined process, VA loans hold the potential to unlock doors to valuable opportunities and empower veterans to achieve their homeownership dreams in the vibrant landscape of Chicago.

Remember: It's crucial to consult with a qualified mortgage professional experienced in VA loans. They can provide personalized guidance, navigate the complexities of the program, and ensure you are making the best decision for your financial situation.

Chapter 7: Navigating Conventional Loans: The Cornerstone of Chicago Real Estate Investment

For investors venturing into the dynamic Chicago real estate market, conventional loans often serve as the cornerstone of their financial strategy. These readily available loans, offered by various private lenders and not directly backed by the government, offer flexibility and competitive rates, making them a popular choice for a diverse range of investors. However, understanding the nuances of conforming versus jumbo loans, the associated benefits and drawbacks, and the eligibility requirements is crucial for making informed investment decisions.

Conforming vs. Jumbo Loans: Navigating the Landscape

Conventional loans fall into two distinct categories: conforming and jumbo. Conforming loans adhere to loan limits set by the Federal Housing Finance Agency (FHFA) and are typically purchased by Fannie Mae and Freddie Mac,government-sponsored

enterprises. In 2023, the conforming loan limit for a single-family home in Chicago, is $726,200. This limit increases for specific high-cost counties within the broader Chicago metropolitan area.

Jumbo loans exceed the conforming loan limit and are not eligible for purchase by Fannie Mae or Freddie Mac. They are held and serviced directly by the originating lender, leading to a less standardized approach with potential variations in interest rates, fees, and eligibility requirements.

Benefits of Conventional Loans:

Flexibility: Compared to government-backed options like FHA loans, conventional loans offer greater flexibility. Investors have more options in terms of loan terms, down payment amounts, and eligible property types,allowing them to tailor the loan to their specific investment goals and financial situation.

Competitive Rates: Conventional loans typically boast lower interest rates than government-backed loans,especially for borrowers with strong credit scores and low debt-to-income ratios. This translates to lower monthly mortgage payments, improving cash flow and potentially increasing investment returns.

Faster Closing Times: The streamlined approval process associated with conforming loans often leads to faster closing times compared to government-backed loans. This can be advantageous in a competitive market where quick action is critical to securing desired properties.

Wide Availability: Due to their widespread use, conventional loans are readily available through a vast network of lenders, providing investors with diverse options when choosing a mortgage provider.

Drawbacks of Conventional Loans:

Higher Down Payment: Conventional loans typically require a higher down payment compared to government-backed loans. While the minimum can be as low as 3% for qualified borrowers, it is often substantially higher,especially for jumbo loans. This can pose a challenge for investors with limited upfront capital.

Stricter Eligibility Requirements: Conventional loans have stricter eligibility requirements compared to government-backed loans, including higher

minimum credit score requirements and lower debt-to-income ratio thresholds. As a result, some investors may not qualify for a conventional loan, limiting their financing options.

Property Requirements: Conventional loans have stricter property appraisal requirements compared to government-backed loans. This can lead to potential delays in the approval process if the property does not meet the lender's standards. Additionally, certain property types, such as fixer-uppers, may not be eligible for conventional financing.

Eligibility Requirements:

To qualify for a conventional loan, investors must meet specific eligibility requirements established by the lender. These typically include:

Credit Score: Investors need a minimum credit score, usually ranging from 620 to 740 or higher, depending on the loan amount and lender requirements.

Debt-to-Income Ratio: A healthy debt-to-income ratio, typically not exceeding 43%, is crucial. This

ensures the borrower's ability to manage mortgage payments alongside other financial obligations.

Employment History: Stable and verifiable employment history demonstrating sufficient income to support mortgage payments is essential.

Down Payment: Investors must provide a minimum down payment, the amount varying based on the loan type and their financial situation.

Property Appraisal: The property must meet the lender's appraisal standards and be located in an eligible area.

Understanding the Choice:

For investors navigating the Chicago real estate market, a thorough understanding of conventional loans is essential.Analyzing the benefits and drawbacks, comparing conforming and jumbo options, and assessing their eligibility is crucial for making informed decisions. Consulting with a qualified mortgage professional experienced in conventional loans can provide invaluable guidance and ensure investors secure the most advantageous financing for their Chicago real estate ventures.

Remember: The information provided in this chapter serves as a general overview and may not encompass all the nuances of conventional loans. Specific requirements and terms can vary depending on the chosen lender and individual circumstances. Always consult with a qualified financial professional for personalized advice and ensure the chosen loan aligns with your specific investment goals and financial situation.

Chapter 8: Portfolio Loans: Unlocking Investment Opportunities in Chicago's Dynamic Real Estate Landscape

Savvy real estate investors navigating the dynamic Chicago market find portfolio loans a compelling alternative to traditional financing options. Unlike conforming loans with rigid guidelines set by government-sponsored enterprises, portfolio loans reside under the originating lender's umbrella, offering greater flexibility and access to larger loan amounts. This opens a door to unique investment opportunities unavailable with conventional loans. Understanding the characteristics, uses, and eligibility requirements of portfolio loans, as well as their potential advantages and drawbacks, is crucial for investors seeking to leverage this powerful tool in their Chicago real estate ventures.

Expanding Investment Horizons:

Unburdened by the strictures of conforming loans, portfolio loans grant investors greater flexibility in terms of loan terms, including:

Larger loan amounts: Portfolio loans often exceed conforming loan limits, enabling investors to acquire more expensive properties or purchase multiple properties simultaneously, significantly expanding their portfolio.

Non-traditional property types: Portfolio loans can be used to finance a broader range of investments beyond traditional single-family homes. This includes commercial properties, mixed-use buildings, and even fixer-uppers, broadening investment opportunities and allowing investors to capitalize on niche market segments.

Flexible repayment options: Tailored repayment options like interest-only periods or balloon payments can improve cash flow management and optimize investment strategies.

These advantages make portfolio loans particularly suitable for experienced investors with diverse portfolios and specific investment goals. They are often utilized for:

Acquiring high-value properties: Securing expensive properties in desirable locations, maximizing potential returns on investment.

Building a diversified portfolio: Diversifying portfolios and mitigating risk by financing multiple properties with a single loan.

Investing in non-traditional properties: Accessing niche market opportunities like commercial real estate or fixer-uppers, which can offer high returns with strategic management.

Meeting the Criteria:

Obtaining a portfolio loan typically requires a stronger financial profile compared to conventional loans. Investors must demonstrate:

Substantial investment experience: Proven track record of success in real estate investment is a prerequisite.

High net worth: A solid net worth and substantial assets demonstrate the investor's ability to repay the loan and manage risks.

Strong credit history: A high credit score and responsible financial management are essential.

Detailed business plan: A well-defined business plan outlining the investment strategy, projected cash

flow, and exit strategy is crucial to convince lenders of the loan's feasibility.

Due to the personalized nature of portfolio loans, specific requirements and documentation may vary depending on the lender and the individual investor's profile. Consulting a qualified mortgage professional experienced in portfolio loans is vital to understand the specific requirements and prepare a compelling application.

Weighing the Advantages and Drawbacks:

Portfolio loans' flexibility and larger loan amounts come with both advantages and drawbacks that investors must carefully consider:

Advantages:

Increased investment opportunities: Access to a broader range of properties and investment strategies, allowing investors to capitalize on unique market opportunities.

Larger loan amounts: Financing significantly higher-value properties or purchasing multiple properties simultaneously to accelerate portfolio growth.

Flexible terms: Customized loan terms like interest-only periods or balloon payments for improved cash flow management and optimized investment returns.

Faster closing times: Portfolio loans often have faster approval processes compared to conventional loans, allowing investors to act quickly on promising opportunities.

Drawbacks:

Stricter eligibility requirements: High net worth, substantial investment experience, and a strong credit history are typically required, making it a less accessible option for some investors.

Higher interest rates: Portfolio loans commonly carry higher interest rates than conventional loans, increasing financing costs and potentially reducing profit margins.

Limited lender availability: Portfolio loans are not offered by all lenders, requiring investors to research and compare options from a smaller pool of potential lenders.

Less standardized terms: The personalized nature of portfolio loans can lead to variations in terms and conditions, making it crucial to carefully review and understand the specific loan agreement before proceeding.

Making the Informed Choice:

Experienced real estate investors can find portfolio loans a powerful tool for acquiring high-value properties, diversifying their portfolio, and capitalizing on unique investment opportunities in the Chicago market. However, due to the stricter eligibility requirements, higher interest rates, and limited lender availability, carefully considering these factors before embarking on this financing route is crucial. Consulting with a qualified mortgage professional experienced in portfolio loans is essential to assess individual eligibility, determine the most advantageous loan terms, and navigate the complexities of these loans to maximize success in Chicago's dynamic real estate landscape.

Chapter 9: Navigating Mortgage Insurance: Understanding the Costs and Benefits in Chicago Real Estate Investment

For real estate investors in Chicago, navigating the complexities of mortgage financing requires a keen grasp of various fees and associated costs. One such crucial element is mortgage insurance (MI), which impacts both monthly payments and overall investment profitability. This chapter delves into the different types of MI, analyzes their benefits and drawbacks, and explores available cancellation options, empowering investors with the knowledge necessary to make informed financial decisions.

Understanding the Different Types of Mortgage Insurance:

Understanding the various types of MI is essential for making informed investment decisions. In the Chicago market, investors typically encounter three primary types:

1. Private Mortgage Insurance (PMI):

PMI is applicable to conventional loans when the down payment falls below 20% of the purchase price.

The cost of PMI varies based on the loan-to-value (LTV) ratio and credit score. Generally, a higher LTV ratio and lower credit score lead to higher PMI premiums.

PMI benefits lenders by providing additional security, enabling investors to qualify for conventional loans with lower down payments, ultimately increasing investment affordability.

The drawback of PMI is that it increases monthly mortgage payments, impacting cash flow and potentially reducing investment returns.

2. FHA Mortgage Insurance Premium (MIP):

MIP is required for all FHA loans, regardless of the down payment amount.

The cost of MIP comprises two components: an upfront mortgage insurance premium (UFMIP) and an annual mortgage insurance premium (MIP). Typically, the UFMIP is 1.75% of the base loan amount, while the annual MIP varies based on the loan term and LTV ratio.

MIP benefits investors by enabling access to FHA loans with lower down payment requirements, making homeownership more attainable for many.

The drawback of MIP is that it increases the overall cost of the loan, impacting profitability. Additionally, FHA loans often have

stricter eligibility requirements and lower loan limits compared to conventional loans.

3. VA Funding Fee:

The VA Funding Fee applies to VA loans, which are available to eligible veterans and service members.

The cost of the VA Funding Fee varies based on the down payment amount and whether it is a first-time use of the VA loan program. This fee can be financed into the loan amount or paid upfront.

The VA Funding Fee benefits investors by providing a one-time cost instead of ongoing monthly payments, potentially saving investors money over time.

The drawback of the VA Funding Fee is that it increases the overall upfront cost of the loan, potentially impacting affordability.

Analyzing the Benefits and Drawbacks of Mortgage Insurance:

The decision to utilize mortgage insurance requires careful consideration of both its benefits and drawbacks. On the one hand, MI provides lenders with greater security, allowing investors to qualify for loans with lower down payments. This can be particularly beneficial for first-time investors or those looking to invest in multiple properties simultaneously.

Additionally, MI can potentially increase investment returns by allowing investors to leverage their capital more efficiently.

However, MI also adds to the overall cost of the loan, impacting monthly payments and potentially reducing the investor's profit margin. Furthermore, some types of MI, such as FHA MIP, come with additional fees and restrictions that can impact affordability and investment flexibility.

Exploring Mortgage Insurance Cancellation Options:

Several strategies exist for reducing or eliminating MI costs. For investors utilizing PMI, reaching a 20% LTV ratio through property appreciation or additional down payments allows them to request PMI cancellation, potentially leading to significant savings on future mortgage payments. Additionally, some lenders offer PMI cancellation options based on specific criteria, such as creditworthiness and timely mortgage payments.

For FHA loans, cancellation options are more limited. Currently, only borrowers who put down at least 10% and made all mortgage payments on time for 11 years can request MIP cancellation.

Making Informed Decisions:

Navigating MI necessitates careful consideration of individual investment goals and financial circumstances. Understanding the different types of MI, their associated costs, and available cancellation options is crucial for making informed decisions.

Consulting with a qualified mortgage professional familiar with the Chicago market can significantly assist investors in selecting the optimal financing solution for their specific needs and maximizing their investment returns.

By carefully analyzing the benefits and drawbacks of MI and exploring available cancellation options, investors can make well-informed decisions that align with their long-term financial objectives and contribute to successful real estate ventures in the dynamic Chicago market.

Chapter 10: Paying Mortgage Insurance Upfront: A Strategic Approach for Homebuyers

When purchasing a home, especially with less than a 20% down payment, most buyers are required to pay for mortgage insurance (MI). This insurance protects the lender in case the borrower defaults on the loan. While traditionally paid as a monthly premium, paying mortgage insurance upfront can be a financially savvy move for some homebuyers. This chapter explores the benefits and implications of this approach, supported by three illustrative examples.

Understanding Upfront Mortgage Insurance

Upfront mortgage insurance is a lump-sum payment made at the closing of the mortgage. This payment covers the insurance policy for a set period or, in some cases, the life of the loan. The upfront cost is typically a percentage of the loan amount and varies based on the loan type and the borrower's credit profile.

Benefits of Upfront Payment

Reduced Monthly Payments: By paying mortgage insurance upfront, borrowers can lower their monthly mortgage payments, making the loan more affordable in the long term.

Interest Savings: Paying upfront means the insurance cost is not subject to interest over the life of the loan, leading to overall savings.

Tax Deductions: In some cases, upfront mortgage insurance can be tax-deductible. However, tax laws vary, so consulting with a tax professional is essential.

Considerations

Initial Cash Outlay: This option requires a significant amount of cash at closing, which might not be feasible for all buyers. This could deplete savings or necessitate taking on additional debt.

Opportunity Cost: The upfront money could be invested elsewhere, potentially earning a higher return than the savings from lower monthly mortgage payments.

Limited Flexibility: Paying upfront MI locks the borrower into the loan terms, potentially making it difficult to refinance or sell the house early without incurring additional fees.

Missing Out on PMI Cancellation: Some lenders offer PMI cancellation options based on specific criteria, such as reaching a certain loan-to-value ratio or maintaining a good credit score. By paying upfront, the borrower may miss out on the opportunity to have their PMI canceled later.

Examples of Upfront Mortgage Insurance

Example 1: Conventional Loan with Private Mortgage Insurance (PMI)

Scenario: John buys a home for $300,000 with a 10% down payment. He opts for a conventional loan with PMI.

Upfront PMI Payment: The lender offers an upfront PMI rate of 2% of the loan amount. John pays $5,400 upfront (2% of $270,000).

Benefit: John's monthly payments are lower without the recurring PMI charge, saving him money over the loan's term.

Example 2: FHA Loan with Upfront Mortgage Insurance Premium (UFMIP)

Scenario: Sarah opts for an FHA loan to purchase a $250,000 home with a 3.5% down payment.

Upfront MIP Payment: FHA loans require an upfront MIP of 1.75% of the loan amount. Sarah pays $4,222.50 upfront (1.75% of $241,250).

Benefit: The upfront MIP reduces her monthly loan payment, though she still pays a monthly MIP due to her low down payment.

Example 3: VA Loan with Upfront Funding Fee

Scenario: Michael, a veteran, buys a home using a VA loan, which doesn't require mortgage insurance but has an upfront funding fee.

Upfront Funding Fee: The fee amount depends on the down payment and the borrower's military status. Assuming Michael pays no down payment and is a first-time user, he pays a 2.3% fee, amounting to $6,900 on a $300,000 loan.

Benefit: This upfront fee eliminates the need for mortgage insurance, significantly reducing Michael's monthly housing cost.

Paying mortgage insurance upfront can be a beneficial strategy for homebuyers who can afford the initial outlay and plan to stay in their homes for the long term. It reduces the monthly mortgage payment and can lead to significant interest savings over the life of the loan. However, it's crucial to weigh the upfront costs against potential future scenarios like early sale or refinancing of the home and consider seeking advice from a qualified mortgage advisor or financial planner. They can help buyers make an informed decision that aligns with their individual financial goals and circumstances.

Before deciding whether paying mortgage insurance upfront is the right option for you, consult with a qualified mortgage professional. They can analyze your financial situation, explain the different MI options available, and help you determine the best course of action to meet your needs.

Chapter 11: Mortgage Buydowns in Real Estate Investment

Understanding and leveraging mortgage buydowns can be a crucial tool for both buyers and sellers. This chapter delves into the intricacies of this financing strategy, exploring its types, benefits, drawbacks, cost considerations, and real-world applications.

Understanding Mortgage Buydowns

A mortgage buydown, in essence, is a financial maneuver that alters the interest rate equation of a mortgage. By making an upfront payment, the borrower can temporarily reduce their interest rate for a specific period, typically the initial years of the loan. This results in lower monthly payments during that period, making the property more affordable and enhancing its market appeal.

Types of Mortgage Buydowns

Several types of mortgage buydowns exist, each catering to different financial objectives. The most common include:

2-1 Buydown: This option reduces the interest rate by 2% in the first year and 1% in the second, before reverting to the original rate for the remaining term.

3-2-1 Buydown: Offering a longer period of reduced payments, this buydown lowers the interest rate by 3% in the first year, 2% in the second, and 1% in the third, before settling at the agreed-upon rate for the remaining years.

Custom Buydowns: Tailored to individual needs, these buydowns can involve different percentage reductions and durations based on negotiation and financial feasibility.

Benefits and Drawbacks: Weighing the Strategic Implications

The primary advantage of employing a mortgage buydown lies in its ability to lower monthly payments, particularly during the initial years of the loan. This benefit resonates especially in markets like Chicago, where property values are high and affordability concerns are paramount. Additionally, buydowns can:

Attract buyers: In a competitive market, offering a buydown can make a property more attractive and increase its selling potential.

Improve cash flow: Lower initial payments can free up cash for investors to invest in other property improvements or manage ongoing expenses.

Strategic refinancing: By leveraging the buydown period, investors can stabilize the property and potentially refinance at a lower rate later.

However, it's crucial to consider the drawbacks associated with this strategy:

Upfront cost: The initial investment required to buy down the rate can be substantial, particularly for larger mortgages or longer buydown periods.

Limited impact on long-term costs: While reducing monthly payments in the short term, buydowns do not impact the overall interest paid over the life of the loan.

Refinancing restrictions: Certain buydown agreements may restrict the borrower's ability to

refinance within the buydown period, potentially limiting future financial flexibility.

Cost Considerations: Understanding the Financial Implications

The cost of a mortgage buydown is directly related to the loan amount, the buydown type, and the agreed-upon interest rate reduction. Generally, the higher the reduction and the longer the period, the greater the upfront cost. This cost is calculated by determining the difference in interest payments between the buydown rate and the original rate for the designated period. This difference is then paid upfront at closing.

Who Pays for the Buydown? A Matter of Strategy

The responsibility for paying the buydown cost can fall on either the buyer or the seller, depending on the individual circumstances and negotiation.

Seller-funded buydown: In a buyer's market, where sellers compete for buyers, offering a buydown can be a strategic incentive to increase the property's appeal and expedite the sale.

Buyer-funded buydown: Buyers may choose to pay for a buydown to lower their initial payments, particularly if they plan to hold the property for the long term or anticipate limited income in the early years.

Examples: Putting Theory into Practice

To illustrate the practical application of mortgage buydowns, consider the following scenarios:

Example 1: Enticing Buyers in a Competitive Market

A $500,000 condominium in Chicago is listed for sale in a highly competitive market. The seller chooses to offer a 2-1 buydown on a 30-year mortgage with a 5% interest rate. This reduces the interest rate to 3% in the first year and 4% in the second year, making the monthly payments significantly lower and attracting a potential buyer who might otherwise be priced out.

Example 2: A Long-Term Investment Strategy

An investor purchases a multi-unit building in Chicago for $750,000. To enhance cash flow and stabilize the property, they opt for a 3-2-1 buydown on their

30-year mortgage at a 6% interest rate. This allows them to:

Generate higher initial rental income: Lower monthly payments free up additional cash that can be reinvested in the property or used for other business ventures.

Accelerate property improvement: With increased cash flow, the investor can expedite necessary repairs and upgrades, enhancing the property's value and rental potential.

Refinance at a favorable rate: By strategically timing the end of the buydown period with improved property valuation and potential interest rate drops, the investor can potentially refinance at a lower rate, securing long-term savings.

Example 3: Seller-Funded Buydown in a Slow Market

In a market experiencing slower sales activity, a seller of a $600,000 property chooses to offer a 2-1 buydown to attract buyers. This strategy involves:

Increased market appeal: The buydown makes the property more competitive compared to others in the market, potentially leading to faster offers and sale closure.

Improved negotiating leverage: The seller can leverage the buydown offer to negotiate other aspects of the sale, such as closing costs or contingencies.

Faster access to proceeds: By expediting the sale, the seller can access the proceeds sooner and reinvest them into other opportunities.

Conclusion: Navigating the Strategic Landscape of Mortgage Buydowns

Mortgage buydowns, when employed strategically, can be a valuable tool for both buyers and sellers in the Chicago real estate market. By understanding the different types, their financial implications, and the potential benefits and drawbacks, investors can leverage this financing approach to achieve their specific investment goals. Whether it's securing a competitive edge in a crowded market, managing initial financial burdens, or enhancing long-term cash flow, mortgage buydowns offer a flexible solution for

navigating the dynamic landscape of Chicago real estate.

Additional Considerations: A Deeper Dive

Before implementing a mortgage buydown strategy, it's crucial to consider the following:

Financial goals: Clearly define your investment objectives and determine whether a buydown aligns with your desired outcome.

Market conditions: Analyze the current market trends and assess the potential impact of a buydown on your selling or buying power.

Alternatives: Explore other financing options and compare them to buydown costs to determine the most cost-effective approach.

Tax implications: Consult with a tax professional to understand the potential tax implications of a buydown, as it may affect itemized deductions.

Long-term plan: Consider the long-term impact of the buydown on your overall financial plan, including

potential refinancing strategies and future investment goals.

By thoroughly evaluating these factors and seeking professional guidance, investors can make informed decisions regarding mortgage buydowns and navigate the complexities of the Chicago real estate market with strategic foresight.

Chapter 12: Banks and Mortgage Lenders – The Pillars of Traditional Financing

In the realm of real estate investment, traditional financing methods, particularly through banks and mortgage lenders, form the bedrock of many investors' strategies. This chapter delves into the intricacies of engaging with these financial institutions, exploring how they operate, the variety of mortgage products they offer, and the ways in which investors can leverage these relationships to finance their real estate ventures in Chicago.

Understanding the Role of Banks and Mortgage Lenders

Banks and mortgage lenders are central to the real estate financing landscape. They provide the capital necessary for investors to purchase and develop properties. Although banks offer a range of financial services, mortgage lenders typically specialize in real estate loans. Both institutions assess the creditworthiness of borrowers and the viability of real estate projects before approving loans.

Types of Financial Institutions

1. Retail Banks:

These are the traditional banks that offer a wide range of services including savings accounts, personal loans, and mortgages. They cater to the general public and have extensive branch networks. While convenient for everyday banking needs, retail banks often have less competitive mortgage rates and may offer a narrower range of loan products compared to specialized mortgage lenders.

2. Mortgage Banks:

Specialized in home loans, these institutions often offer a broader range of mortgage products compared to retail banks. They may also have more flexible underwriting guidelines and the expertise to handle complex loan applications. Additionally, mortgage banks often focus on building relationships with real estate professionals, including investors, which can expedite the loan process.

3. Credit Unions:

Member-owned financial cooperatives, credit unions can offer lower interest rates and fees than traditional banks due to their non-profit structure. However, membership eligibility may be restricted to specific groups, such as employees of certain companies or residents of particular communities. This can limit their accessibility for some investors.

Exploring the Spectrum of Mortgage Products

Banks and mortgage lenders offer a variety of loan products, each tailored to different types of real estate investments and borrower profiles. Understanding these options is crucial for investors to choose the loan that best aligns with their needs and financial goals.

1. Fixed-Rate Mortgages:

These are the most traditional form of home loans, where the interest rate remains constant over the life of the loan. They offer stability in monthly payments, which is a significant advantage for investors who

value predictability and long-term planning. However, fixed-rate mortgages typically have higher initial interest rates compared to adjustable-rate mortgages.

2. Adjustable-Rate Mortgages (ARMs):

ARMs begin with a fixed interest rate for a specific period, after which the rate adjusts at predetermined intervals based on market conditions. This can be a beneficial option for investors who are comfortable with potential interest rate increases or for short-term investments where the loan will be paid off before significant adjustments occur. However, the uncertainty associated with future interest rate fluctuations can pose a risk for long-term investments.

3. Jumbo Loans:

For property investments that exceed the loan limits set by government-sponsored entities, such as Fannie Mae and Freddie Mac, jumbo loans are a viable option. These loans typically have higher interest rates and stricter qualification criteria due to the increased risk involved. However, they offer

increased borrowing power for investors seeking larger properties.

4. Government-Insured Loans:

These loans, including FHA, VA, and USDA loans, are designed for specific borrower categories, such as first-time homebuyers, veterans, or individuals living in rural areas. They often come with lower down payment requirements and more flexible underwriting guidelines compared to conventional loans. However, they may have higher interest rates and mortgage insurance premiums.

5. Construction Loans:

For investors embarking on development projects, construction loans provide the financing needed to purchase land, build structures, and complete renovations. These loans are typically short-term and require ongoing progress reports and inspections to ensure project completion.

Navigating the Loan Application Process

Applying for a mortgage involves several steps:

1. Pre-Approval:

This initial step provides investors with an estimate of how much they can borrow based on their financial information. It involves submitting basic financial documents and obtaining a credit report review. Pre-approval helps investors focus their search on properties within their budget and provides reassurance to sellers that they are qualified buyers.

2. Application:

The formal application process requires detailed financial documentation, including income tax returns, bank statements, and debt verification. This information is used by the lender to assess the borrower's creditworthiness and the viability of the loan.

3. Underwriting:

During this phase, the lender performs a thorough review of the application materials and supporting documents. They may request additional information or clarification from the borrower. The underwriter assesses the risk of the loan and determines whether to approve the loan based on pre-established guidelines.

4. Approval and Closing:

Once the loan is approved, the borrower and lender schedule a closing date.

Once the loan is approved, the borrower and lender schedule a closing date. At closing, the final paperwork is signed, including the mortgage note, deed of trust, and other legal documents. The loan funds are then disbursed to the seller, and the property ownership is transferred to the borrower.

Building Relationships with Lenders: A Strategic Advantage

Establishing strong relationships with banks and mortgage lenders can offer several advantages for real estate investors:

1. Better Terms:

For borrowers with a solid track record and a strong working relationship with a lender, the potential for more favorable loan terms, including lower interest rates and fees, increases significantly.

2. Personalized Service:

Lenders who know and trust an investor are more likely to provide personalized service and quicker response times to their inquiries and needs. This can be invaluable when navigating complex situations or encountering unexpected challenges.

3. Flexibility:

Established relationships can lead to increased flexibility from lenders. This may be particularly

beneficial during challenging economic times when borrowers need to renegotiate loan terms or require additional financing for repairs or improvements.

4. Access to Exclusive Products:

Some lenders offer exclusive mortgage products not readily available to the general public. Building relationships can provide access to these specialized options, potentially tailored to specific investment strategies or financial objectives.

Navigating Challenges and Risks: A Proactive Approach

While traditional financing offers numerous opportunities for real estate investors, it is not without its challenges and risks:

1. Interest Rate Fluctuations:

Changes in interest rates can significantly impact the cost of borrowing, especially for adjustable-rate mortgages. Investors should carefully consider the potential impact of rising rates and have a contingency plan in place.

2. Strict Qualification Criteria:

Banks and lenders have stringent criteria for loan approval, including minimum credit score requirements, debt-to-income ratios, and down payment requirements. Investors with less-than-perfect credit or limited financial resources may face challenges in obtaining traditional financing.

3. Property Approval:

The property itself must meet certain standards and pass an appraisal for the loan to be approved. Investors should be aware of potential issues with the property that could hinder their ability to secure financing.

4. Closing Costs:

In addition to the down payment, closing costs associated with traditional financing can be substantial, including loan origination fees, appraisal

fees, and title insurance. Investors should budget for these additional expenses.

5. Market Downturns:

Economic downturns can impact real estate values, potentially leading to negative equity or defaults. Investors should carefully consider the market conditions and their risk tolerance before securing a loan.

Leveraging Traditional Financing for Real Estate Success

Banks and mortgage lenders play a crucial role in the financing of real estate investments. Understanding the range of mortgage products they offer, the intricacies of the loan application process, and the importance of building strong lender relationships are fundamental to navigating the real estate investment landscape.

While traditional financing offers numerous opportunities for investors, it also requires a keen understanding of the associated challenges and risks.

By mastering these aspects, investors can effectively leverage traditional financing options to build and grow their real estate portfolios in a strategic and sustainable manner.

Chapter 13: Navigating Loan Programs and Guidelines in Real Estate Investment

The intricate tapestry of real estate investment demands a thorough understanding of the diverse loan programs available and their accompanying guidelines. This chapter delves into this crucial aspect, particularly focusing on the Chicago market. We'll explore the nuances of various loan programs, their eligibility criteria, benefits, limitations, and alignment with distinct investment strategies.

Navigating the Loan Program Landscape:

The realm of real estate financing offers a plethora of loan programs, each tailored to specific investment objectives. From government-backed options to conventional mortgages, every program comes with a unique set of rules and guidelines governing eligibility, application, and repayment.

Government-Backed Loans:

These loans, insured by federal agencies, often offer favorable terms like lower down payments and less stringent credit requirements. Popular options include:

FHA Loans: Guaranteed by the Federal Housing Administration, these loans appeal to first-time homebuyers due to their low down payment requirements.

VA Loans: Backed by the Department of Veterans Affairs, these loans cater to veterans and active military personnel, offering benefits like no down payment and no private mortgage insurance (PMI).

USDA Loans: Supported by the United States Department of Agriculture, these loans are designed for rural property buyers, offering zero down payment options.

Conventional Loans:

These are mortgage loans not insured by any government agency. Typically offered by private lenders, they require higher credit scores and down

payments compared to government-backed loans. Two common types include:

Fixed-Rate Mortgages: Offering a stable and predictable interest rate for the entire loan term, these provide consistent monthly payments.

Adjustable-Rate Mortgages (ARMs): These start with a fixed interest rate for an initial period, after which the rate adjusts periodically based on market trends.

Jumbo Loans:

Exceeding the conforming loan limits set by the Federal Housing Finance Agency, jumbo loans are designed for financing luxury properties and high-value investments. They often require stringent credit qualifications and significant down payments.

Understanding Loan Program Guidelines:

Each loan program comes with meticulously crafted guidelines dictating who can borrow, for what purpose, and under what terms. These guidelines

ensure responsible lending practices and mitigate risks for both the lender and borrower.

Eligibility Criteria:

Credit Score Requirements: Most loan programs have minimum credit score requirements. Government-backed loans are generally more forgiving, while conventional and jumbo loans demand higher scores.

Income and Employment Verification: Lenders require proof of stable income and sufficient employment history to ensure borrowers have the capacity to meet their loan obligations.

Debt-to-Income Ratio (DTI): This measures a borrower's monthly debt payments against their income. Lower DTI ratios demonstrate a greater ability to manage loan repayments.

Property Appraisals and Inspections:

Appraisals: Lenders require an appraisal to confirm the property's value justifies the loan amount. This is particularly crucial in markets like Chicago, where property values can vary significantly.

Inspections: Some programs, especially FHA and VA loans, require specific property inspections to ensure the property meets safety and quality standards.

Loan-to-Value Ratio (LTV):

The LTV ratio measures the loan amount against the property's value. Lower LTV ratios imply greater equity in the property and lower risk for the lender.

Aligning Loan Programs with Investment Strategies:

Choosing the right loan program is a strategic decision that should be aligned with your overall investment plan.

Long-Term Hold Investors: Fixed-rate conventional loans might be the better choice due to their stable payments over the long term.

Flippers and Short-Term Investors: ARMs or bridge loans might be more suitable, offering lower initial interest rates, which can benefit investors planning to sell or refinance quickly.

Investors in Rural Properties: USDA loans can provide significant advantages, including no down payment options.

Navigating the diverse landscape of loan programs and understanding their accompanying guidelines is paramount for navigating the world of real estate investment. In a dynamic market like Chicago, selecting the right loan program aligned with your investment strategy can significantly impact your venture's success. Each program offers distinct advantages and limitations, and thorough comprehension of these nuances is essential. By equipping yourself with this knowledge, you can make informed decisions about loan programs that enhance your investment portfolio and contribute to your long-term financial goals.

Chapter 14: Credit Scores and Loan Eligibility in Real Estate Investment

In the dynamic landscape of real estate investment, particularly in a market as vibrant as Chicago, understanding the impact of credit scores on loan eligibility is paramount. This chapter explores the intricacies of credit scores, their influence on securing financing, and strategies for improving this crucial aspect of your financial profile.

The Role of Credit Scores in Real Estate Financing

A credit score acts as a numerical representation of an individual's creditworthiness, based on their credit history. It plays a vital role in the loan approval process, influencing the terms and conditions offered by lenders. A strong credit score can open doors to better loan options, lower interest rates, and a smoother path to securing financing for your real estate investments.

Decoding Credit Score Ranges

Credit scores typically range from 300 to 850, with higher scores indicating better credit health. Generally, they are categorized as follows (Consumer Financial Protection Bureau, 2023):

- Excellent: 750 and above
- Good: 700-749
- Fair: 650-699
- Poor: 600-649
- Very Poor: below 600

Each category comes with its own set of challenges and opportunities in acquiring real estate financing.

Factors Influencing Credit Scores

Several factors contribute to shaping your credit score, including:

Payment History: Timeliness of credit payments (Federal Trade Commission, n.d.)

Credit Utilization: Ratio of current credit debt to the total available credit limit (Experian, 2023)

Length of Credit History: Duration of active credit usage (Federal Trade Commission, n.d.)

Types of Credit in Use: The mix of credit accounts, such as credit cards, mortgages, and student loans (Experian, 2023)

New Credit Inquiries: Frequency of applying for new credit (Experian, 2023)

Impact of Credit Scores on Real Estate Financing

Credit scores not only influence loan approval but also determine the interest rate and other loan terms offered by lenders.

Loan Approval

Lenders use credit scores to assess the risk associated with lending money. A higher score indicates a lower risk, making it easier to get approved for real estate loans. Conversely, a lower score might require alternative financing options or stricter loan terms (Federal Housing Finance Agency, 2023).

Interest Rates and Loan Terms

Your credit score directly impacts the interest rate offered on loans. Higher scores typically translate to lower interest rates, resulting in significant savings over the life of a real estate loan. Additionally, favorable scores can lead to more flexible loan terms, such as lower down payments and more lenient repayment options (Federal Trade Commission, n.d.).

Strategies to Enhance Your Credit Score

Maintaining or improving one's credit score is crucial for real estate investors. Here are some effective strategies to boost your creditworthiness:

Regular Monitoring and Reporting Errors: Regularly check your credit reports for any inaccuracies that might be pulling your score down. Errors can range from incorrect account information to fraudulent activities (Federal Trade Commission, n.d.).

Managing Debt Efficiently: Keep credit card balances low and prioritize paying off existing debts to improve your credit utilization ratios and boost your credit score (Federal Trade Commission, n.d.).

Make Timely Payments: Ensure all credit payments are made on time. Late payments can have a significant negative impact on your credit score (Experian, 2023).

Diversify Your Credit Types: A healthy mix of different types of credit accounts, such as credit cards, mortgages, and student loans, can positively affect your credit score by demonstrating your ability to manage multiple credit lines responsibly (Experian, 2023).

Credit Scores in the Chicago Real Estate Market

It is essential to understand how local lenders in Chicago view credit scores when navigating the city's real estate market. While general credit score principles apply, local market conditions and individual lender preferences might influence loan approval processes and terms.

Conclusion

In conclusion, credit scores play a pivotal role in shaping the trajectory of your real estate investment journey. They are key indicators of your financial health and risk for lenders, influencing both the availability and cost of real estate financing. For investors in the Chicago real estate market, a comprehensive understanding of credit score dynamics, coupled with proactive credit management strategies, is key to unlocking financing opportunities and achieving long-term investment success.

References:

Consumer Financial Protection Bureau. (2023, October 12). What is a credit score? Consumer Financial Protection Bureau. https://www.nerdwallet.com/article/finance/credit-score-ranges-and-how-to-improve

Experian. (2023, October 24). What is a credit report and why is it important

Chapter 15: The Loan Application Process in Real Estate Investment

Navigating the loan application process holds paramount importance, especially in a market like Chicago. This chapter delves into the intricacies of securing real estate financing, guiding investors through each stage, from initial preparations to final approval and disbursement. By comprehending this process, investors can effectively secure the necessary funding to fuel their real estate endeavors.

Preparing for the Loan Application:

1. Assessing Financial Health:

Before embarking on the application journey, investors must meticulously assess their financial standing. This includes a thorough understanding of credit scores, discussed in Chapter 14, as well as evaluating their income, existing debts, and overall financial stability. A robust financial foundation contributes significantly to securing favorable loan terms.

2. Understanding Loan Requirements:

Diverse loan products come with varying requirements. Investors should thoroughly research and understand the eligibility criteria for their desired loan, whether it be a conventional mortgage, a government-backed loan, or a specialized real estate investment loan.

3. Gathering Necessary Documentation:

The application process demands a multitude of documents. Frequently required documents include:

- Proof of income: W-2 forms, tax returns, etc.
- Proof of assets: Bank statements, investment accounts, etc.
- Credit history: Credit reports from major credit bureaus
- Identification documents: Driver's license, passport, etc.

The Loan Application Process:

1. Choosing a Lender:

Selecting the right lender is a critical decision. Investors should evaluate factors beyond simply interest rates and loan terms. Additionally, the lender's reputation, customer service, and familiarity with the Chicago real estate market are crucial considerations.

2. The Application:

The formal application is a request for loan funding. It requires providing personal and financial information, details about the property to be financed, and the intended use of the loan.

3. Loan Estimate:

Following application submission, the lender provides a loan estimate. This document outlines the loan's terms, including the interest rate, monthly payments, and closing costs. Investors should meticulously review this document.

Underwriting and Approval:

1. Credit and Risk Assessment:

The lender meticulously evaluates the applicant's creditworthiness, the property's value (typically requiring an appraisal), and the investment's feasibility. This assessment determines the loan's approval or denial.

2. Conditional Approval:

If the risk assessment is satisfactory, the lender issues a conditional approval. This indicates that the loan is approved, subject to fulfilling specific conditions, such as providing additional documentation or clarifying certain details.

Closing the Loan:

1. Closing Documentation:

At closing, the borrower signs numerous legal documents. These include the mortgage agreement, outlining the loan's terms, and the promissory note, signifying the commitment to repay the loan.

2. Closing Costs:

Closing costs are fees associated with finalizing the loan. These may include appraisal fees, title insurance, and origination fees, among others. Budgeting for these costs is crucial.

3. Disbursement of Funds:

Once all documents are signed and closing costs are paid, the lender disburses the funds. For real estate purchases, the funds typically go directly to the seller.

Post-Closing Considerations:

After closing, the investor's focus shifts towards managing the investment and ensuring timely loan repayments. Maintaining sound financial standing is crucial, as it impacts future borrowing capabilities and overall investment success.

The loan application process is a multifaceted journey, requiring meticulous preparation, informed selection of loan products, close attention to detail throughout the application and underwriting phases, and prudent financial management after closing. For Chicago real estate investors, mastering this process unlocks the financial resources needed to capitalize on investment opportunities and achieve long-term success in the dynamic and competitive real estate market.

References:

- Federal Housing Finance Agency. (2023, October 26). Conforming Loan Limits.https://www.fhfa.gov/DataTools/Tools/Pages/Conforming-Loan-Limit-Map.aspx
- Federal Trade Commission. (n.d.). Credit scores. https://consumer.ftc.gov/articles/credit-scores
- Experian. (2023, October 24). What is a credit report and why is it important?https://www.experian.com/blogs/ask-experian/credit-education/report-basics/my-credit-report/

Chapter 16: Deciphering Mortgage Documentation: A Guide to Understanding Your Loan Paperwork

Navigating the intricate world of real estate investments in a dynamic market like Chicago necessitates a thorough understanding of mortgage documentation. This chapter serves as a guide for investors, demystifying the various documents involved in real estate financing and highlighting key points to focus on. By gaining clarity on these documents, investors can make informed financial decisions and approach the loan process with confidence.

The Significance of Mortgage Documentation:

Mortgage documents constitute the legal foundation of the loan agreement between the lender and the borrower. They meticulously outline the rights and responsibilities of each party, along with the specific terms and conditions governing the loan. Grasping these documents is crucial not only for legal compliance but also for making informed and responsible financial choices.

Key Mortgage Documents:

The mortgage process involves several key documents, each serving a distinct purpose within the loan agreement.

1. Loan Estimate:

Provided within three business days of the loan application, the Loan Estimate offers a preliminary snapshot of the loan's terms. It outlines the estimated interest rates, monthly payments, and closing costs, allowing the borrower to assess the initial financial implications.

2. Promissory Note:

The Promissory Note forms the core of the mortgage documentation. This legally binding document signifies the borrower's commitment to repay the loan under the stipulated terms, including the loan amount, interest rate, payment schedule, and duration.

3. Mortgage or Deed of Trust:

This document acts as collateral for the Promissory Note, granting the lender a lien on the property. It details the lender's rights in case of default, including the ability to proceed with foreclosure.

4. Closing Disclosure:

Received at least three business days before the loan closing, the Closing Disclosure provides the final and detailed terms of the loan. This includes the finalized interest rate, monthly payments, and closing costs. It's crucial to compare this document to the Loan Estimate to identify any changes.

Chicago Deal Flow: Financing Your Real Estate Investment

5. Escrow Statement:

This document details the funds held in escrow for property taxes and insurance. It outlines the charges covered by the escrow account and specifies the amount the borrower needs to contribute monthly to maintain sufficient funds.

Understanding Terms and Conditions:

Each mortgage document is filled with specific terms and conditions that require careful consideration.

1. Interest Rates and Payment Terms:

The Promissory Note details the interest rate of the loan, whether fixed or adjustable, along with the payment terms, including the amount and frequency of payments.

2. Fees and Closing Costs:

The Closing Disclosure provides a comprehensive breakdown of all fees and costs associated with the loan. This includes origination fees, appraisal fees, title insurance, and any other processing fees.

3. Implications of Default:

The Mortgage or Deed of Trust explains what constitutes a default and outlines the lender's rights in such situations, including the possibility of foreclosure.

4. Tax and Insurance Requirements:

Mortgage documentation specifies the requirements for property taxes and insurance. The Escrow Statement, in particular, details how these will be managed and funded.

Special Considerations in Chicago:

The Chicago real estate market has unique local regulations that may impact mortgage documentation. For instance, property taxes in Chicago are generally higher than in other regions, which can affect the Escrow Statement and overall loan costs.

The Role of Legal and Financial Advisors:

Given the complex and legally binding nature of mortgage documentation, consulting with legal and financial advisors is highly recommended. These professionals can provide valuable insights and clarify the terms and implications of the loan paperwork, ensuring investors fully understand their commitments and rights within the agreement.

Conclusion:

Mastering the landscape of mortgage documentation empowers real estate investors, particularly in a dynamic market like Chicago, to navigate the financing process with confidence. Thoroughly understanding each document, from the Loan Estimate to the Closing Disclosure, allows investors to make informed decisions aligned with their investment goals and

ensures legal and financial compliance. By demystifying these documents and seeking professional guidance when needed, investors can approach the loan process with knowledge and clarity, paving the way for successful real estate ventures.

Chapter 17: Hard Money Loans – A Flexible Financing Solution in Real Estate

The dynamic world of real estate investment requires a diverse arsenal of financing tools, especially in a market as vibrant and diverse as Chicago's. Conventional financing options may not always align with the specific needs of every investor, where alternative solutions like hard money loans come into play. This chapter delves into the intricate world of hard money loans, exploring their defining characteristics, the advantages and challenges they present, and their applications in various real estate investment scenarios. By gaining a comprehensive understanding of this alternative financing option, investors can make informed decisions aligned with their individual goals and navigate the diverse landscape of Chicago's real estate market with greater flexibility and confidence.

Defining the Hard Money Loan:

Hard money loans are a type of short-term financing specifically tailored to real estate transactions. Unlike traditional bank loans, which rely on the borrower's creditworthiness and financial history, hard money loans are secured by the underlying real estate property itself and are sourced from private lenders or companies. This unique structure enables faster approval times

and greater flexibility in terms compared to traditional financing options.

Key Characteristics:

Collateral-Based: Unlike credit-driven loans, hard money loans focus on the property's value as the primary security. This allows investors with less-than-perfect credit to access financing, as the focus shifts from credit history to the property's potential.

Shorter Terms: Hard money loans are designed for short-term needs, typically ranging from 1 to 3 years. This aligns with the fast-paced nature of real estate transactions and provides investors with a clear exit strategy.

Higher Interest Rates: Due to the inherent risk associated with shorter terms and collateral-based lending, hard money loans often have higher interest rates compared to traditional loans. However, the potential return on investment can offset this cost for investors with a well-defined strategy.

Faster Funding: The approval process for hard money loans is streamlined and efficient, allowing for quick access to funds. This can be crucial for time-sensitive real estate deals, enabling investors to seize opportunities and capitalize on market trends.

Applications of Hard Money Loans:

Hard money loans play a vital role in various real estate investment scenarios, offering a valuable alternative to traditional financing options.

Property Flipping: For investors who buy and renovate properties to sell for a profit, hard money loans provide the necessary short-term funding to acquire, renovate, and flip properties quickly, maximizing return on investment.

Financing Unique Properties: Traditional loans might not be available for certain properties considered "non-standard" due to their condition, type, or location. Hard money lenders offer greater flexibility and can finance properties that fall outside the purview of conventional financing.

Overcoming Credit Challenges: Investors with credit issues may find it difficult to secure traditional financing. Hard money loans offer a viable alternative, allowing access to capital and enabling them to participate in attractive investment opportunities.

The Process of Obtaining a Hard Money Loan:

Securing a hard money loan involves a distinct process compared to traditional financing:

Property Evaluation: The lender conducts a thorough evaluation of the property to determine its value and set the loan amount.

Term Negotiation: The borrower and lender negotiate the terms of the loan, including interest rates, repayment schedule, and loan duration.

Approval and Funding: Once approved, the loan funds are typically disbursed quickly, allowing investors to move forward with their investment plans.

Advantages and Challenges:

While hard money loans offer distinct advantages, they also come with specific challenges that investors need to consider:

Advantages:

Speed and Flexibility: The streamlined approval process and flexible terms allow investors to act quickly and adapt to changing market conditions.

Access to Investment Opportunities: Hard money loans unlock opportunities that might be inaccessible through traditional financing, offering a broader range of investment options.

No Credit Score Dependence: Investors with less-than-perfect credit history can still access funding, enabling them to participate in the market.

Challenges:

Higher Costs: Hard money loans typically carry higher interest rates and fees, impacting the overall cost of capital.

Short Repayment Period: The short-term nature of these loans requires investors to have a clear strategy for repayment and exit within the stipulated timeframe.

Risk of Property Loss: Failure to repay the loan can lead to the lender seizing the property as collateral,resulting in significant financial loss.

Hard Money Loans in the Chicago Market:

Within the competitive and diverse landscape of Chicago's real estate market, hard money loans offer a valuable tool for investors navigating a wide range of property types and investment strategies. From single-family homes in need of renovation to unique commercial spaces, hard money loans can provide the necessary capital to secure and capitalize on promising investment opportunities quickly and efficiently.

Chapter 18: Private Equity and Crowdfunding: Unleashing Capital for Chicago Real Estate

Navigating the Landscape of Private Equity and Crowdfunding:

In the dynamic and competitive environment of Chicago real estate investment, both private equity and crowdfunding offer compelling options for investors seeking alternative financing solutions. Carefully considering the advantages and challenges of each approach, coupled with thorough research and due diligence, is crucial for making informed investment decisions.

Key Considerations for Investors:

Investment Goals: Clearly define your investment goals and risk tolerance to determine which approach aligns best with your strategy.

Financial Resources: Assess your available capital and ensure it aligns with the minimum investment requirements of your chosen platform or fund.

Risk Appetite: Evaluate your comfort level with risk and choose an option that matches your risk tolerance.

Investment Horizon: Consider your investment timeline and select an option that aligns with your desired investment duration.

Platform and Fund Selection: Conduct thorough research on available platforms and funds, scrutinizing their track records, investment philosophies, and fee structures.

Deal Evaluation: Analyze the specific projects or investments offered, assessing their financial viability, market potential, and potential returns.

Professional Guidance: Consider seeking professional guidance from financial advisors or real estate experts to navigate the complexities of private equity and crowdfunding investments.

The Future of Alternative Financing in Chicago Real Estate:

As the Chicago real estate market evolves, private equity and crowdfunding are poised to play an increasingly significant role in shaping its future. These innovative approaches offer new avenues for capital allocation, broadening investor participation and unlocking opportunities beyond the reach of traditional financing models. With their continued growth and development, private equity and crowdfunding are expected to further democratize real estate investment, making it more accessible and inclusive for individuals seeking to capitalize on the vibrant and dynamic Chicago market.

Conclusion:

Private equity and crowdfunding represent powerful tools for investors seeking to tap into the lucrative Chicago real estate market. By understanding the distinctive mechanisms of each approach, carefully weighing their advantages and challenges, and conducting thorough due diligence, investors can unlock new opportunities for diversification, capital appreciation, and passive income generation. As these innovative financing solutions continue to evolve, their impact on the Chicago real estate landscape will only become more pronounced, paving the way for a more inclusive and accessible investment environment, where capital flows freely and fuels the ongoing growth and development of the Windy City.

Chapter 19: Seller Financing and Lease-to-Own Options – Innovative Paths to Real Estate Ownership

The journey of real estate investment extends beyond the realm of conventional financing methods. While bank loans and mortgages remain dominant, innovative and viable alternatives emerge in certain scenarios, particularly within the diverse and evolving market of Chicago. Seller financing and lease-to-own options present themselves as such alternatives, offering unique pathways to property ownership. This chapter delves into the mechanics, advantages, and considerations surrounding these unconventional yet increasingly popular financing strategies.

Understanding Seller Financing:

Seller financing, also known as owner financing, occurs when the seller of a property transforms into the lender. Instead of the buyer acquiring a loan from a traditional financial institution, the seller extends credit directly to the buyer, enabling the purchase of the property.

The Mechanics of Seller Financing:

Under a seller financing arrangement, the buyer and seller engage in negotiations to establish the terms of the loan, including the interest rate, repayment schedule, and consequences of potential default. The buyer then makes

payments to the seller in accordance with these agreed-upon terms. A promissory note typically documents the loan details, while a mortgage or deed of trust serves as security for the loan, securing it against the property itself.

Advantages of Seller Financing:

Flexible Terms: Seller financing offers the advantage of customizable terms, allowing both the buyer and seller to tailor the agreement to their specific needs and circumstances.

Simpler Transaction: Compared to the complexities involved in traditional bank financing, the seller financing process can be more straightforward and streamlined, potentially accelerating the closing process.

Accessibility for Buyers: This option opens doors for buyers who may not qualify for conventional loans due to credit challenges or other financial constraints, offering an alternative route to property ownership.

Considerations for Seller Financing:

Risk for Sellers: When opting for seller financing, sellers take on the inherent risks associated with lending, including the possibility of buyer default and the potential for delayed or missed payments.

Property Control: Sellers must be aware that they retain a vested interest in the property until the loan is

fully repaid, limiting their ability to sell the property freely during this period.

Legal and Financial Advice: Both parties are advised to seek expert guidance from legal and financial professionals to ensure the fairness of the agreement and its compliance with relevant legal regulations.

Exploring Lease-to-Own Options:

Lease-to-own, also known as rent-to-own, involves a structured contract where the tenant rents a property with the option to purchase it at a predetermined price in the future. This arrangement combines a standard lease agreement with a dedicated purchase option, providing the tenant with the flexibility to explore ownership over time.

Structure of Lease-to-Own Agreements:

A typical lease-to-own agreement functions as a hybrid of a traditional lease and a purchase option. Tenants pay rent, with a portion potentially allocated towards the eventual purchase of the property. The agreement clearly outlines the lease duration, the purchase price, and the specific terms under which the tenant can exercise the purchase option.

Benefits of Lease-to-Own:

Building Credit and Savings: This arrangement allows tenants to utilize the lease period to improve their credit scores and

accumulate funds for a down payment, strengthening their financial position for eventual ownership.

Testing the Property: Tenants have the opportunity to reside in the property and assess its suitability before committing to a full purchase.

Fixed Purchase Price: The purchase price is typically agreed upon upfront, providing tenants with security and protection against potential market fluctuations.

Challenges of Lease-to-Own:

Non-Refundable Option Fees: Tenants often pay an upfront option fee, which is non-refundable even if they choose not to purchase the property later.

Risk of Lost Investment: If the tenant decides not to exercise the purchase option, they may lose the portion of the rent allocated towards the purchase, representing a potential financial loss.

Market Volatility: Fluctuations in the real estate market can pose risks. If property values decline, the tenant might be locked into an agreement to purchase at a higher price than the market value at the time of exercise.

Seller Financing and Lease-to-Own in Chicago:

In Chicago's dynamic real estate landscape, characterized by diverse property types and varying market conditions, these alternative financing methods hold significant appeal. They offer viable pathways to homeownership and investment, particularly in areas where traditional financing might be challenging or in neighborhoods undergoing revitalization processes.

Legal and Financial Implications:

Both seller financing and lease-to-own agreements require careful consideration from a legal and financial perspective. Contracts must be meticulously drafted to safeguard the interests of both parties and ensure compliance with all relevant state and local real estate laws. Consulting with qualified real estate attorneys and financial advisors is crucial for both buyers and sellers navigating these agreements.

Seller financing and lease-to-own options represent innovative and versatile tools for navigating the complex world of real estate investment, particularly within the diverse market of Chicago. By understanding the mechanics and nuances of these alternative methods, weighing the potential benefits and risks, and seeking informed guidance, investors and homebuyers can unlock new opportunities for ownership and participation in the vibrant Chicago real estate landscape.These creative approaches offer pathways to property ownership that may not be readily available through traditional financing channels, enabling

individuals to invest in their future and contribute to the continued growth and development of the city. As these alternative financing strategies continue to gain traction and evolve, they hold the potential to democratize real estate ownership, making it more accessible and inclusive for a wider range of individuals seeking to build wealth and achieve their investment goals.

Chapter 20: Understanding Loan Terms and Interest Rates in Real Estate Financing

Navigating the Crossroads of Finance: Loan Terms and Interest Rates in Real Estate Investment

In the dynamic and intricate world of real estate investment, particularly in a market as vibrant and diverse as Chicago's, a comprehensive understanding of loan terms and interest rates is paramount. These fundamental elements serve as the cornerstone of any successful real estate financing strategy, directly influencing not only the immediate financial obligations but also the long-term financial trajectory of any investment. This chapter delves into the intricacies of loan terms and interest rates, providing a clear and concise analysis of their significance, how they work, and their impact on real estate investment in the Chicago market.

The Indispensable Role of Loan Terms:

Comprising the parameters and conditions under which a loan is granted and repaid, loan terms form the bedrock of any real estate financing decision. They define not just the immediate financial obligations but also the long-term fiscal implications of an investment, impacting the overall cost of capital and profitability.

Chicago Deal Flow: Financing Your Real Estate Investment

Dissecting the Loan Term:

The loan term, essentially the timeframe within which the loan is to be repaid, varies significantly depending on the investment strategy and the property itself. Short-term loans, ranging from a few years to a decade, are often utilized for properties intended for flipping or quick refinancing, whereas long-term loans, spanning 15 to 30 years or more, cater to buy-and-hold investment strategies. The chosen loan term significantly affects the monthly payment amount, the total interest paid over the life of the loan, and the overall financial viability of the investment.

Interest Rates: The Driving Force:

The interest rate charged on a loan acts as the primary driver of its cost, directly influencing the profitability of any real estate investment. A deeper understanding of its impact is crucial for making informed financial decisions.

Navigating the Interest Rate Landscape:

Two primary types of interest rates dominate the real estate financing landscape:

Fixed-Rate Mortgages: These loans offer stability and predictability, featuring an interest rate that remains constant throughout the loan term. This stability facilitates financial planning and budgeting, as monthly payments remain consistent.

Adjustable-Rate Mortgages (ARMs): In contrast, ARMs introduce an element of flexibility, offering lower initial rates compared to fixed-rate mortgages. However, the interest rate fluctuates over time, adjusting based on market conditions. This introduces uncertainty and potential financial volatility into the equation.

Factors Shaping Interest Rates:

Several key factors influence the interest rates offered by lenders:

- **Market Conditions:** Economic factors such as inflation, Federal Reserve policies, and the health of the housing market directly impact interest rates.
- **Credit Score:** Individuals with strong credit scores typically qualify for lower interest rates due to the perceived lower risk of default.
- **Down Payment:** Making a larger down payment can often secure a lower interest rate by reducing the lender's risk exposure.
- **Loan Type:** Government-backed loans, such as FHA or VA loans, often come with different interest rates compared to conventional loans.

Demystifying Loan Payments:

Calculating loan payments accurately is crucial for budgeting and investment planning. The loan amount, interest rate, and term, along with property taxes, insurance, and potentially

private mortgage insurance (PMI), all play a role in determining the total monthly payment.

Amortization: Spreading the Cost:

Amortization refers to the process of paying off a loan over time through regular installments. An amortization schedule outlines exactly how each payment is allocated between interest and principal reduction, providing a clear picture of how the loan balance is gradually paid down.

Chicago Market Dynamics:

In the diverse and dynamic Chicago real estate market, characterized by varying property values and investment opportunities, choosing the optimal loan terms and securing an advantageous interest rate are critical aspects of any successful investment strategy.

Local Market Insights:

Investors need to remain informed about local economic conditions, property tax rates, and the competitive lending landscape in Chicago, as these factors significantly influence the availability and affordability of financing options.

Leveraging Expert Guidance:

Working with mortgage professionals and financial advisors who possess a deep understanding of the Chicago market can provide

invaluable insights into securing favorable loan terms and interest rates, ultimately enhancing the success of an investment strategy.

The intricate interplay between loan terms and interest rates serves as a cornerstone of any successful real estate investment strategy. Investors navigating the dynamic Chicago market must possess a clear understanding of these elements and their impact on the financial viability of their investments. By carefully considering these factors, ideally with the guidance of qualified professionals, investors can make informed financing decisions that align with their investment goals and optimize their return on investment.

Chapter 21: Negotiating Favorable Loan Agreements in Real Estate Investment

Navigating the competitive landscape of Chicago real estate requires more than just identifying promising properties—it demands mastery in the art of securing favorable loan agreements. This chapter delves into the intricacies of loan negotiation, equipping you with the knowledge and strategies to craft agreements that align perfectly with your investment goals.

Beyond the Bargaining Table: Understanding the Loan Landscape

Effective negotiation transcends mere haggling over interest rates. It's about understanding the entire spectrum of a loan agreement, from terms and fees to underlying conditions. By dissecting each element, you can strategically build towards an agreement that empowers your investment objectives.

Key Elements of Loan Agreements:

Interest Rates: While prominent, they're just one piece of the puzzle. Consider the loan term's impact on monthly payments and overall interest costs.

Loan Term: This duration influences both your financial obligations and your investment timeline.

Amortization Schedule: This blueprint dictates how your payments will be allocated between principal and interest throughout the loan's life.

Prepayment Penalties: Be mindful of clauses that penalize early loan repayment, potentially impacting your exit strategy.

Closing Costs: These encompass fees for processing, underwriting, and other administrative services. Negotiate where possible to minimize upfront expenses.

Preparation: The Foundation of Successful Negotiation

Before stepping into the negotiation arena, thorough preparation is your most potent weapon.

Market Research and Leverage:

Current Market Rates: Understanding Chicago's current market rates and terms empowers informed discussions.

Multiple Loan Offers: Gather competing offers to leverage in negotiations, demonstrating your attractive borrower profile.

Strengthening Your Position:

Credit Score: A stellar credit score bolsters your negotiation power.

Solid Financials: Having your financial statements in order showcases your reliability as a borrower.

Seek Expert Guidance:

Financial Advisors: Their insights can clarify which terms are negotiable and realistic.

Mortgage Brokers: Their local knowledge and connections can unlock hidden opportunities.

Negotiation Tactics and Strategies: Artfully Shaping the Agreement

Effective negotiation requires a delicate balance of tact, knowledge, and strategic maneuvering.

Flexibility and Trade-offs:

Identify the elements crucial to your investment strategy and where you can be flexible. Swapping a longer loan term for a lower interest rate might be a viable option.

Cultivating Relationships:

Building rapport with lenders can unlock favorable terms. Regular communication and demonstrating reliability can go a long way.

Clear Communication:

Articulate your investment plans and how they align with the loan you seek. A well-defined strategy inspires confidence in lenders.

Leveraging the Market:

Use competing offers as bargaining chips. Showing alternative options incentivizes lenders to improve their proposals.

Legal Considerations:

Ensure all negotiated terms are secured in writing within the loan documents. Consulting a legal professional can prevent future disputes.

Contingencies: Safeguarding Your Investment

Negotiate contingencies, like clauses that adjust terms based on future events (e.g., market fluctuations), to provide flexibility and protect your investment.

Case Studies: Lessons from Chicago's Real Estate Landscape

Examining real-life scenarios where Chicagoland investors successfully negotiated favorable loan agreements can provide practical insights for your own endeavors.

The Chicago Factor:

Tailor your negotiation strategies to Chicago's unique market dynamics. Understanding local trends and lender preferences can be the key to securing optimal terms.

Negotiating favorable loan agreements is a crucial skill in real estate investing, empowering you to maximize the return on your investment. By delving into the loan landscape, preparing diligently, and employing strategic negotiation tactics, you can unlock advantageous terms that propel your Chicago real estate ventures to success. Remember, the competitive market demands continuous learning and adaptation of your negotiation strategies. Stay informed, refine your skills, and conquer the art of crafting agreements that fuel your investment goals.

This revised version incorporates your proposed changes, aiming for improved clarity, conciseness, and impact. Feel free to further adapt it to your specific needs and preferences.

Chapter 22: Closing the Deal and Funding Your Investment: Navigating the Final Steps in Real Estate Financing

Reaching the pinnacle of your real estate investment journey – closing the deal – demands meticulous attention to detail. It's a crucial and intricate stage, where the months of planning and negotiations culminate in securing your property and funding your dream. This chapter equips you with the knowledge and insights to navigate the final steps of financing your real estate venture, particularly within the dynamic landscape of Chicago's market.

Understanding the Closing Process:

Closing, often referred to as settlement or escrow, marks the final act in purchasing and financing a property. It's the culmination of all legal and financial procedures, ensuring a smooth transfer of ownership.

Preparing for Closing: A Multi-Pronged Approach

1. **Ensuring Loan Approval:** Confirm all mortgage conditions are met, and the loan is ready for disbursement.
2. **Title Search and Insurance:** Conduct a thorough title search to verify no legal claims exist on the property, and secure title insurance for future protection.

Chicago Deal Flow: Financing Your Real Estate Investment

3. **Home Inspection and Appraisal:** Complete any required inspections and an appraisal to confirm the property's value and condition.
4. **Document Review:** Carefully scrutinize every closing document, including the loan agreement, to ensure accuracy and understanding of terms.

Key Participants in the Closing Orchestra:

1. **Escrow Agent:** Coordinates the closing process, acting as the neutral third-party holding funds and documents until all conditions are met.
2. **Real Estate Attorney:** Provides legal counsel and reviews all contractual documents to safeguard your interests.
3. **Lender Representative:** Ensures loan-related documents are accurate and funds are disbursed promptly.
4. **Real Estate Agents:** Represent both the buyer and seller, navigating the sale with expertise.

The Role of Escrow: Adding a Layer of Security

An escrow account serves as a secure vault for funds and crucial documents, held until all closing conditions are satisfied. This neutral third-party involvement adds a layer of security and ensures a smooth transaction for all parties.

Managing Escrow Funds: Where Does the Money Go?

1. **Down Payment and Closing Costs:** Your down payment and closing costs are typically held in escrow until the deal closes.
2. **Property Taxes and Insurance:** In some cases, escrow accounts manage ongoing property tax and insurance payments as part of your mortgage agreement.

Navigating Closing Costs: A Matter of Dollars and Cents

Closing costs encompass a range of fees and expenses associated with finalizing your real estate transaction. While they can vary based on the property and deal specifics, understanding their composition is crucial.

Typical Closing Cost Categories:

1. **Loan Origination Fees:** Charged by the lender for processing your mortgage.
2. **Title Insurance and Search Fees:** Protect against future claims on the property title.
3. **Appraisal and Inspection Fees:** Cover the costs of property valuation and any required inspections.
4. **Attorney's Fees:** For legal representation throughout the closing process.
5. **Recording Fees:** Charged by local authorities to officially record the transaction.

Estimating and Negotiating Closing Costs:

1. **Loan Estimate:** Provided by the lender, this document outlines the expected closing costs.
2. **Negotiation Opportunities:** Some closing costs may be negotiable, and in certain cases, the seller may even agree to contribute to them.

Finalizing the Deal: The Moment of Truth

Closing day is the culmination of your investment journey. Here's what to expect:

1. **Document Review and Signing:** All parties meticulously review and sign the necessary legal and financial documents.
2. **Fund Disbursement:** The lender disburses the loan funds, covering the property purchase price and closing costs.
3. **Recording of the Sale:** The transaction is officially documented with local authorities, transferring ownership to you.

Post-Closing Considerations: Beyond the Finish Line

With the closing behind you, several important steps remain:

1. **Mortgage Payments:** Understand your payment schedule and ensure timely remittances.

2. **Property Management:** Decide whether you'll manage the property yourself, hire a professional, or utilize it for personal use.
3. **Long-Term Financial Planning:** Integrate your investment into your broader financial goals and strategies.

Closing in the Chicago Market: Local Nuances

Chicago's vibrant real estate market may have specific closing procedures, such as variations in property tax rates or recording fees. Familiarizing yourself with these local aspects is key to a smooth closing experience.

Closing the deal and securing your real estate investment marks a significant achievement. By meticulously planning, preparing, and understanding the intricacies of the closing process, you can navigate this crucial stage with confidence. Remember, in Chicago's dynamic market, mastering these final steps is key to successfully securing and managing your property for long-term success.

Chapter 23: Demystifying Closing Costs in Your Chicago Real Estate Purchase

In the thrilling journey of real estate investment, navigating the financial landscape can be as exhilarating as it is intricate. One key aspect, often shrouded in mystery, is the realm of closing costs. Understanding these hidden expenses, particularly within the vibrant and dynamic Chicago market, is crucial for a smooth and successful investment. This chapter delves into the intricacies of closing costs, dissecting their components, their significance, and strategies for effectively managing them.

The Essence of Closing Costs: Beyond the Price Tag

Closing costs are not simply an add-on to the property price – they're the necessary fees and expenses incurred by both buyers and sellers during the transfer of ownership. These costs are separate from the purchase price and typically paid at the closing of the real estate transaction, marking the culmination of months of planning and negotiation.

Dissecting the Components: A Cost Breakdown

While closing costs can vary depending on the property, location, and deal specifics, some common components are frequently encountered:

Loan Origination Fees: Charged by the lender for processing your new loan, paving the way for your investment.

Title Insurance: A crucial safeguard, protecting both you and the lender from any legal issues with the property's title.

Appraisal Fees: Ensuring the property's fair market value is accurately assessed, protecting all parties involved.

Inspection Fees: From structural checks to environmental assessments, these fees provide valuable insights into the property's condition.

Attorney Fees: Legal expertise throughout the transaction, ensuring your interests are represented and protected.

Escrow Fees: The neutral third-party facilitating the closing process, ensuring a smooth and secure transaction.

Recording Fees: Officially registering the new deed and mortgage with local authorities, solidifying your ownership.

Survey Fees: Verifying property lines and ensuring accurate boundaries for your future investment.

Credit Report Fees: The lender's cost of assessing your creditworthiness and determining loan eligibility.

Chicago Deal Flow: Financing Your Real Estate Investment

Prorated Property Taxes: Covering the portion of the year's property taxes already paid by the seller, ensuring fair division of expenses.

Understanding Chicago's Nuances: Local Twists

While the core components of closing costs remain similar across the country, Chicago's unique real estate market presents some specific considerations:

Transfer Taxes: Both local and state transfer taxes apply to real estate transactions in Chicago. Understanding these taxes and who is responsible for them is crucial for accurate budgeting.

Property Type Variations: From single-family homes to towering commercial buildings, the diverse range of properties in Chicago can significantly influence closing cost amounts.

Negotiation Opportunities: While not all fees are set in stone, certain closing costs in Chicago, like transfer taxes, may offer some negotiation potential between buyer and seller.

Managing the Costs: Strategies for Smart Investors

Effectively navigating closing costs can significantly impact your overall investment strategy. Here are some key strategies for cost-conscious investors:

Seek Cost-Effective Options: Shop around for services like title insurance, inspections, and surveys. Comparing prices and seeking competitive quotes can save you money.

Negotiation Power: Don't be afraid to negotiate! Some closing costs, like seller contributions or lender fees, can be negotiable.

Utilize Loan Estimates: Carefully review the Loan Estimate provided by your lender, as it outlines the expected closing costs. This document can help you plan and budget accordingly.

Closing Cost Calculators: Online calculators offer a preliminary estimate of closing costs based on your property and location. While not exact, they provide a valuable starting point for planning.

Seek Expert Advice: Consider consulting real estate agents and financial experts for accurate cost estimates and informed negotiation strategies. Their local knowledge and expertise can be invaluable in the dynamic Chicago market.

The Path to Informed Investment

Closing costs, while often overlooked, are an inherent element of real estate transactions. Understanding and effectively managing these costs in Chicago's diverse market is crucial for ensuring the success of your investment. By demystifying the components, employing cost-saving strategies, and seeking professional advice, you can navigate the closing process with confidence and pave the way for a profitable and successful real estate venture.

Remember, in the ever-evolving landscape of Chicago's real estate, knowledge and preparation are your most potent assets.

Chapter 24: Building Your Dream Team: Navigating Chicago Real Estate with Expert Support

In Chicago's dynamic real estate market, navigating the intricacies of financing and investment is rarely a solo act. To truly thrive in this competitive landscape, you need more than just ambition – you need a strong, collaborative team by your side. This chapter dives into the essential roles within your investor team, highlighting their expertise, and equipping you with the guidance to assemble a powerhouse unit that empowers your investment journey.

Why Collaboration is Key:

Real estate investment is a multifaceted beast, encompassing tasks that range from market analysis to financial acrobatics, legal hurdles, and property management. A well-rounded team brings diverse skillsets and perspectives to the table, fostering informed decision-making and boosting your chances of success. Think of them as your real estate compass, guiding you through uncharted territory and ensuring your financial ship stays afloat.

The A-Team of Real Estate Investment:

Real Estate Agent: Your local market guru, navigating the complex web of listings, properties, and neighborhood nuances. They'll sniff out promising opportunities, negotiate like champions, and keep you ahead of the curve.

Mortgage Expert: Your financial maestro, understanding the intricacies of loans and mortgages. They'll translate financial jargon, secure the best rates, and ensure your investment dream aligns with your financial reality.

Real Estate Attorney: Your legal guardian, protecting you from pitfalls and ensuring every transaction is squeaky clean. They'll dissect contracts, navigate legalese, and safeguard your investments from unforeseen legal storms.

Financial Advisor: Your financial navigator, charting a course towards financial stability. They'll analyze risks,optimize tax strategies, and help you make sound financial decisions for the long haul.

Property Manager (optional): Your rental property maestro, taking the reins of day-to-day operations. They'll find tenants, handle maintenance, and keep your investment generating consistent income.

Insurance Agent: Your risk shield, providing peace of mind from unforeseen events. They'll assess your property's needs,

recommend suitable coverage, and ensure you're protected from the unexpected.

Assembling Your Dream Team:

Finding the right players for your team isn't just about checking boxes. It's about aligning expertise with your investment goals and fostering a collaborative, communicative environment.

Demonstrated Expertise: Choose professionals with a proven track record of success in their respective fields, especially those familiar with the nuances of the Chicago market.

Investment Alignment: Ensure your team understands and champions your investment goals, whether you're chasing long-term rental income, flipping houses, or venturing into commercial real estate.

Communication Champions: Effective communication is the lifeblood of any team. Choose professionals who are responsive, transparent, and keep you informed at every stage of the process.

Trustworthy Navigators: Building a successful real estate journey requires trust. Choose individuals you can rely on for sound advice, ethical practices, and unwavering support.

Building a Winning Culture:

A strong team isn't just a collection of individuals; it's a well-oiled machine where collaboration thrives.

Open Communication: Encourage regular communication, both within the team and with yourself. This fosters transparency, builds trust, and ensures everyone is on the same page.

Defined Roles and Responsibilities: Clearly define each team member's role and responsibilities to avoid confusion and overlap. This creates a smooth workflow and ensures everyone is contributing their unique expertise.

Mutual Respect and Trust: Cultivate an environment of respect and trust where everyone feels comfortable sharing their ideas and opinions. This fosters creativity, innovation, and ultimately, better investment decisions.

Continuous Learning: The real estate landscape is constantly evolving. Encourage your team to stay updated on the latest trends, regulations, and best practices. This ensures your knowledge base remains sharp and your investment strategies stay ahead of the curve.

Leveraging Your Team's Power:

Your team isn't just there to hold your hand; they're active participants in your investment decisions.

Market Analysis and Property Selection: Involve your real estate agent and other team members in analyzing market trends, identifying promising properties, and assessing potential risks and rewards.

Financial and Loan Planning: Work closely with your mortgage expert and financial advisor to secure financing that aligns with your investment strategy and financial capabilities.

Legal Compliance and Risk Management: Rely on your real estate attorney and insurance agent to navigate legal complexities, minimize risks, and ensure your investments are protected.

Tech-Powered Collaboration:

Embrace technology as your team's secret weapon. Utilize project management tools, communication platforms, and data analysis software to streamline communication, share information, and make informed decisions collectively.

Conclusion:

A strong investor team is the cornerstone of successful real estate investing. In the competitive and diverse market of Chicago, having a team of skilled, experienced, and aligned professionals can make a significant difference in your investment journey. By carefully selecting your team members and fostering a collaborative and respectful working environment, you can enhance your investment success and navigate the complexities of real estate financing and management with greater confidence and efficiency.

Chapter 25: Mastering the Art of Property Management: Securing Your Chicago Investment

Owning an investment property in Chicago unlocks a world of opportunity, but alongside the potential for profit comes the responsibility of effective management. In this dynamic market, success hinges on knowledge, strategy, and a proactive approach. This chapter delves into the intricacies of property management, equipping you with the tools and insights to maximize your return and safeguard your investment.

Understanding the Property Management Landscape:

Managing an investment property isn't simply collecting rent. It's a multi-faceted endeavor encompassing tenant relations, maintenance oversight, financial stewardship, and legal compliance – each element woven together to preserve and enhance the value of your asset.

Essential Responsibilities: Your Roadmap to Success:

Tenant Management: Finding reliable tenants is key. This involves thorough screening, clear lease agreements, efficient rent collection, and prompt responses to their needs.

Maintenance and Repairs: Regular upkeep is paramount. Proactive inspections, timely repairs, and occasional upgrades

keep your property competitive and prevent costly issues down the line.

Financial Management: Profitability is the goal. Set realistic rental rates, track expenses meticulously,maximize tax benefits, and ensure financial transparency.

Legal Compliance: Ignorance is not bliss. Stay informed about local housing regulations, landlord-tenant laws,and safety codes. Failure to comply can be costly.

Navigating the Path to Success:

Effective property management demands both strategic planning and operational efficiency. Here are some key tactics for your Chicago investment journey:

Leveraging Professional Expertise: Consider hiring a property manager, especially if you lack local knowledge,juggle multiple properties, or simply seek a hands-off approach.

Building Positive Tenant Relations: Attract and retain quality tenants through clear communication, prompt issue resolution, and a fair approach. Happy tenants translate to stable income and fewer headaches.

Proactive Maintenance and Upkeep: Don't wait for problems to arise. Schedule regular inspections, encourage tenant communication about maintenance needs, and prioritize preventative measures.

Chicago Deal Flow: Financing Your Real Estate Investment

Financial Savvy and Tax Optimization: Stay in control of your finances. Budget accurately, track expenses meticulously, and maximize tax benefits available for rental properties.

Staying Ahead of the Legal Curve: Knowledge is power. Familiarize yourself with Chicago's specific regulations, tenant rights, and building codes. Partner with legal professionals for complex situations.

Challenges and Market Fluctuations: Navigating the Storm:

Property management isn't always smooth sailing. Be prepared for:

Difficult Tenants: Develop strategies for handling challenging situations, including tenant eviction procedures.

Unforeseen Repairs: Budget for unexpected expenses and prioritize essential repairs promptly.

Market Fluctuations: Stay informed about economic trends and adjust your strategy as needed to maintain competitiveness.

Chicago's Unique Landscape: Adapting Your Approach:

Chicago's diverse neighborhoods and dynamic market present specific challenges and opportunities:

Understanding Local Market Dynamics: Rental rates, tenant demographics, and maintenance costs can vary significantly

across Chicago. Research your specific neighborhood to set competitive rates and market your property effectively.

Navigating Chicago's Legal Maze: Stay informed about Chicago-specific regulations, such as tenant eviction processes, lead paint inspections, and licensing requirements.

Building a Network of Local Experts: Partner with experienced property managers, legal professionals, and contractors who understand the intricacies of the Chicago market.

Conclusion:

Effective property management is an ongoing journey, requiring continuous learning, strategic adaptation, and a commitment to excellence. By understanding the responsibilities, employing the right strategies, and adapting to the unique demands of Chicago's market, you can transform your investment property into a stable source of income and build a solid foundation for long-term success. Remember, in this dynamic landscape, knowledge and proactive management are your most valuable assets. So, take the reins, embrace the challenges, and watch your Chicago investment flourish.

Chapter 26: Conquering Risks in Real Estate: Safeguarding Your Chicago Investment

Chicago's real estate market, with its dynamic pulse and diverse landscapes, offers alluring opportunities for investment. But with every venture comes the inevitable dance with risk. To waltz with confidence and protect your investment dreams, you need a strategic, risk-aware approach. This chapter equips you with the knowledge to identify potential pitfalls and the tools to navigate them with grace.

Unveiling the Risk Landscape:

Real estate investment, like a vibrant tapestry, is woven with threads of varying risks. Market fluctuations, financial pitfalls, operational challenges, and legal hurdles can all threaten your investment journey. Recognizing these risks is the first step towards mitigating them.

Market Fluctuations: The Ever-Changing Tide:

Chicago's real estate market is a dynamic beast, susceptible to economic shifts, supply-demand imbalances, and the ever-changing tides of interest rates. Understanding these fluctuations and their potential impact on property values, rental income, and the overall investment climate is crucial for informed decision-making.

Financial Risks: Taming the Cash Flow Beast:

Financing your investment can be a double-edged sword. Rising interest rates, mortgage payment challenges, and refinancing hurdles can all threaten your financial stability. Robust financial analysis, maintaining a healthy reserve fund, and utilizing leverage prudently are essential safeguards against these financial storms.

Operational Risks: Keeping Your Investment Ship Afloat:

Day-to-day property management presents its own set of challenges. Tenant issues, unexpected repairs, and maintenance needs can all disrupt your investment journey. Proactive maintenance, effective tenant screening, and reliable local partnerships can help weather these operational storms.

Legal Hurdles: Navigating the Labyrinth of Laws:

Non-conformity with local, state, and federal laws can be a costly misstep. Zoning regulations, building codes,landlord-tenant laws, and legal disputes can all pose significant risks. Staying informed, seeking legal counsel when needed, and maintaining compliance are your shields against these legal labyrinths.

Strategizing for Risk Mitigation:

Now that you understand the risks, let's equip you with the tools to mitigate them:

Chicago Deal Flow: Financing Your Real Estate Investment

Diversify your investments: Spread your wings across different property types, locations, and even markets. This reduces your vulnerability to localized risks.

Conduct thorough market research: Before diving in, delve deep into Chicago's diverse neighborhoods and economic trends. Knowledge is your compass in navigating market fluctuations.

Utilize leverage prudently: Leverage can amplify both gains and losses. Use it strategically, keeping financial stability at the forefront.

Maintain a healthy financial buffer: Unexpected expenses are inevitable. Build a reserve fund to weather financial storms and maintain cash flow stability.

Screen tenants meticulously: Careful tenant selection reduces the risk of rent loss and property damage.

Prioritize property maintenance: Regular upkeep minimizes costly repairs and preserves your investment's value.

Seek professional guidance: Real estate experts, financial advisors, and legal professionals can provide invaluable insights and navigate complex situations.

Chicago's Unique Risk Landscape:

Chicago's vibrant tapestry comes with its own set of risk threads. Seasonal property vacancies, fluctuating property taxes, and

historic preservation regulations are just a few examples. Tailoring your risk management strategies to these unique challenges is crucial for success.

Conclusion:

Risk management is not just a shield; it's a dance you master alongside your investment journey. By understanding the risks, implementing mitigation strategies, and adapting to Chicago's unique market, you can navigate the dance floor with confidence. Remember, in this dynamic game, knowledge, proactive planning, and professional guidance are your most valuable assets. So, step onto the dance floor of Chicago real estate investment, prepared, informed, and ready to waltz with risk and conquer your investment dreams.

Chapter 27: Navigating the Evolving Landscape of Chicago Real Estate Financing

Chicago's real estate market, a dynamic and ever-shifting landscape, is poised for a transformative journey in its financing landscape. Driven by economic shifts, technological advancements, and changing regulatory frameworks, the way investors navigate this crucial aspect of real estate investment is undergoing a profound metamorphosis. Let's delve into the emerging trends, potential challenges, and exciting opportunities shaping the future of real estate financing in this vibrant city.

Emerging Trends: Reshaping the Financing Terrain:

The real estate financing landscape is no longer a static entity. Several key trends are reshaping its future:

Tech-Powered Transformation: Fintech is revolutionizing the sector, streamlining loan applications with digital platforms and enhancing security with innovations like blockchain and AI. Think faster, more accessible financing options.

Demand Shift: Beyond the Brick-and-Mortar Box:
Demographics and evolving lifestyle preferences are influencing investment and financing decisions. Sustainable living, co-living spaces, and alternative living options are gaining traction, creating unique financing opportunities.

Regulatory Evolution: From lending practices to zoning laws and tax policies, regulatory frameworks are adapting to the changing landscape. Investors need to stay informed and adapt their strategies accordingly.

Challenges and Opportunities: A Balancing Act:

The future presents both hurdles and exciting possibilities:

Market Volatility: A Dance with Uncertainty: Economic fluctuations can impact property values and returns. Adaptability and a keen understanding of market trends will be key to navigating this volatility.

Interest Rate Fluctuations: The Cost of Capital: Changes in interest rates can significantly impact borrowing costs. Investors need to be adept at securing favorable terms amidst these fluctuations.

Hidden Gems in Diverse Neighborhoods: Beyond iconic landmarks, Chicago's diverse neighborhoods offer hidden investment gems. Emerging areas, particularly those benefiting from urban revitalization, present promising financing opportunities.

Sustainable and Socially Responsible Investing: A Growing Force:

Green financing options and investments in underserved communities are gaining momentum, reflecting a growing

emphasis on sustainability and social responsibility. Investors seeking impact alongside returns will find this trend increasingly attractive.

Tech Disruption: Embracing the Digital Wave: The future holds further technological disruption. From data-driven market analysis to blockchain-powered transactions, technology will continue to streamline processes and enhance investment decision-making.

Preparing for the Future: Building Your Compass:

To navigate the evolving landscape of Chicago real estate financing, investors need to:

- **Stay Informed:** Market trends, regulatory changes, and technological advancements are crucial to understanding the evolving landscape.
- **Embrace Technology:** Utilize digital tools for efficient analysis, risk assessment, and financing processes.
- **Adapt and Diversify:** Flexibility and adaptability in investment strategies will be key to responding to market changes and capitalizing on emerging opportunities.
- **Build Strong Relationships:** Collaborating with experienced financial advisors and real estate professionals who understand the Chicago market is invaluable for informed decision-making.

The future of real estate financing in Chicago is not a predetermined path, but a dynamic and exciting journey. By staying informed, embracing change, and capitalizing on emerging trends, investors can navigate this evolving landscape with confidence and unlock the potential for success in this vibrant city. Remember, in this ever-shifting terrain, adaptability, knowledge, and a forward-thinking approach will be your most valuable assets. So, grab your compass, embrace the transformation, and prepare to navigate the exciting future of Chicago real estate financing.

About The Author

In the realm of real estate, experience is an invaluable asset.
Michael Linton, a distinguished Broker with a prominent real
estate firm, brings over 37 years of unwavering commitment and
excellence in the industry. His journey is marked by not just
longevity but a consistent drive to help clients achieve their real
estate goals, a dedication that has earned him a reputation as a
top-tier professional.

A Seasoned Real Estate Expert

Michael's illustrious career has been punctuated by exceptional
achievements and a deep understanding of the real estate
landscape. His expertise extends across a wide spectrum, making
him a trusted advisor for both buyers and sellers. Specializing in
the diverse real estate market of Chicago, Michael has honed his
skills to become an adept navigator of this dynamic terrain.

With his guidance, countless clients have found their ideal
properties, whether it's a charming suburban home or a bustling
commercial space in the heart of the city. His

clients have benefited from his in-depth market knowledge, and his extensive experience in negotiating the best deals in this competitive landscape.

Passion for Real Estate Investment

While Michael has an impressive track record in various segments of real estate, his passion shines brightest when it comes to real estate investment. He understands the unique appeal and wealth-building potential of the Chicago real estate market. Michael's expertise in investment strategies has helped numerous clients identify and secure lucrative real estate opportunities in the Windy City and its suburbs.

A Commitment to Excellence

Throughout his career, Michael Linton has been a beacon of commitment to his clients. He understands that real estate transactions are not just about properties; they are about fulfilling dreams and securing financial futures. Michael is dedicated to providing the highest level of customer service, ensuring that his clients feel valued, heard, and supported throughout their real estate journeys. His availability to address questions and concerns, paired with his personalized service, has resulted in loyal clients who return to him time and again.

Connect with Michael Linton on LinkedIn

Join my exclusive LinkedIn community to stay updated on the latest real estate investment trends, insights, and opportunities in Chicago and its suburbs. By connecting with Michael Linton and Linton Global Partners on LinkedIn, you gain access to a wealth of knowledge and a network of like-minded individuals who are passionate about real estate investing.

Michael Linton's LinkedIn Profile:
https://www.linkedin.com/in/lintonglobal/

Subscribe to My Investment Newsletter

Unlock the potential of real estate investment in Chicago by subscribing to my Investment Newsletter. Stay informed about handpicked investment opportunities, market trends, expert insights, and exclusive resources delivered directly to your inbox.

Subscribing is easy and free. Simply visit my website, navigate to the newsletter section, and enter your email address. Join a community of smart investors

who rely on my curated information to make informed investment decisions.

Don't miss out on the chance to connect with industry experts, fellow investors, and valuable resources. Follow us on LinkedIn and subscribe to our newsletter today to embark on your journey to success in Chicago's real estate market.